MARIA COSTELLO
QUEEN OF BIKERS

THE AUTOBIOGRAPHY

MARIA COSTELLO
QUEEN OF BIKERS

THE AUTOBIOGRAPHY

MARIA COSTELLO
WITH STEVE PITTS

To Michael,
Best Wishes,
Maria Costello MBE

Pennant Books

First published in paperback 2010
by Pennant Books

British Library Cataloguing-in-Publication Data:
A catalogue record for this book is available on request from
The British Library

ISBN 978-1-906015-54-1

Design & Typeset by Envy Design Ltd

Printed and bound in the UK by William Clowes, Beccles, NR34 7TL

Pennant Books
A division of Pennant Publishing Ltd
PO Box 5675
London W1A 3FB

www.pennantbooks.com

CONTENTS

PROLOGUE

FUN AND GAMES AT THE PALACE

Tuesday, November 17, 2009. A day I'll never forget. A day that I'd been anticipating for five months would be (fingers crossed) one of the best of my life. A day that I'd spend with royalty, and yet for a few uncomfortable hours it seemed I was going to miss my date with Prince Charles.

It turned out to be the kind of day which sums up my life so far. It began full of optimism and expectation, yet I was soon in tears; I was so frugal that I hadn't booked a hotel; I'd made wrong calls that could have ended in disappointment, not just for me but for my parents and sister; I was in a hurry and late for a date with our Royal Family.

But I also showed initiative, made my parents proud, gave the heir to the throne a laugh and ended the day with the beaming smile that I hope – for all my personal vulnerability – will never be wiped off my face.

It was also a day in which, like most others, I didn't make life simple for myself.

So, why was I meeting the Prince of Wales at Buckingham

Palace? To be made a Member of the Order of the British Empire, of course!

And what had I done to deserve the MBE? You tell me. My initial reaction was that it might have been a wind-up. I've got used to telling people why I *think* I was given the honour, but I honestly have no idea who nominated me, and so I can't really begin to explain why I received my letter of notification, out of the blue, in June 2009.

I'm just an ordinary girl with a passion for motorbikes, who has spent much of her adult life trying – and too often struggling – to be accepted in the male-dominated, often sexist world of motorcycle racing. I was the first female to claim a place on the podium at the famous Isle of Man races, and I'm in *Guinness World Records* as the fastest woman on the TT circuit for five years – although I only got in there once I'd had the record taken away from me.

It may not surprise you to learn that I arrived at the Palace on a motorbike. Some say it was corny, others have claimed it was a PR stunt by a woman trying to keep herself in the news to keep her sponsors happy. My family and friends, the people who know the real me – the often fragile and insecure Maria as opposed to the leather-clad, invincible biker-chick image – were just happy that I'd actually made it to the Palace to receive my award. But it certainly hadn't been planned that way. I only arrived on the back of a motorbike because things had gone wrong.

I'll tell you all about my great Palace escapade later in this book. But for now, let me return to the possible reason why I was honoured. Being one of the few women competing in motorcycle racing has often been fun, occasionally painful, but never easy. I've been racing since 1995 – broken bones and other injuries (there have been plenty) permitting – but the real successes, the moments of triumph that the very top riders measure themselves by, have been few and far between.

I certainly wasn't invited to the Palace to discuss a lengthy list of my victories. In all my days as a senior racer I've only climbed up the podium steps once or twice when competing against the boys. And although I did once win a ladies' series by a massive margin, that event was little more than a condescending tilt to us girls.

Don't forget, this is a sport in which women have traditionally done little more than flash the flesh around the pit-lane – there to be stared at and not heard, unless a horny male rider decides to make your day by hitting on you (which you can be pretty sure of).

I made my race debut as a determined but nervous 21-year-old, and have survived in a sport which often seems to be no more welcoming to female riders than a strip club. If you're in the pit-lane showing off a bit of flesh, you'll hold a biker's attention until the next pretty girl comes along. If you're there to take on the guys at 150mph around twisting circuits, then don't for a moment think that you'll be accepted as anything approaching their equal, because there really is no precedent. But I don't want to sound bitter!!!

This is a testosterone-fuelled sport that has little notion of sexual equality, although things are a little better than when I first took to my race bike. I've been around so long now that guys will acknowledge me in the paddock, and most of the mechanics don't stare quite as blatantly as they once did. I like to think that I no longer get smashed off of the track just because some idiotic male ego can't stand the thought of being beaten by a girl. (Believe me, it has happened.)

But I'm still not taken as seriously as I should be, and nor are any of the other women racers. There's a long, long way to go, and I reckon we'll have only achieved genuine equality when there's as much male eye candy prancing around the pit-lane as there is female.

Perhaps I came to the attention of whoever decides on the honours list because – despite plenty of knocks and broken bones, the frustrating spells of physiotherapy and recovery – I keep jumping back on my bike to show men that women can be just as tough as they are. And believe me, bikers are tough buggers – you don't risk your life at speeds of up to 200 mph on something as unstable as a two-wheeled motorbike if you don't possess mental and physical strength.

If I had to hazard a guess as to my nominee, it would be either the Sports Council of England or the Women's Sports Foundation, two organisations I've been heavily involved with. In working with these bodies, I see it as my duty to try to encourage young girls into sport – although I do cringe when they say they want to be just like me. I also do a bit of charity work (I'm a patron of Riders for Health and Mencap), but no more than many other sportsmen and women.

So I'll probably never know, and perhaps it doesn't matter. The overwhelming majority of people I've spoken with about it have been warmly generous in their congratulations – though I've still had to contend with the odd chauvinist like the guy who tried to set up an online petition to strip me of my MBE, because I supposedly hadn't done anything to deserve it.

That's an extreme example of the hostility that, as a woman, you can encounter in this sport. But I do know that my failure to be treated as an equal – even by some of the men I beat on a regular basis – has often laid bare my basic insecurities, fed my vulnerability and left me tearful and depressed.

As I've got older and become more comfortable in my own skin, I've come to recognise that the guys also suffer the same self-doubt and negative self-image that have often hindered me. This is why anyone different – a female, for example – is seen as a threat that needs quashing.

For many years, the one thing I tried so hard not to do was cry in front of any man, however much they had hurt me physically or mentally. Now, if needs must, I can cry with the best of them – and I see it as a sign of female strength rather than weakness. It gives me an outlet for my emotions that 99% of my fellow competitors can never allow themselves. Yet many could certainly do with it. Just as I continue to strive to beat them at their own game, perhaps a few of them will find some balance in their life by trying to find their feminine side.

CHAPTER 1

IT ALL BEGINS WITH BROKEN BONES

My big day out at Buckingham Palace is probably about as close to a wedding day as anything my parents will ever see with me.

I was born in the maternity unit at Northampton General Hospital on 9 June 1973, weighing only 3lb 10oz, but Mum says I was a natural-born fighter, which I guess was shown shortly after my sister, Tina, was born three years later. Apparently I climbed into her pram and kicked her in the head – a sign of things to come?!

I've had many different relationships over the ensuing decades, but I've never seen myself as the marrying kind. I hope I don't end up regretting it, but give me a choice between a good bike and a good man and it's no choice at all. Motorbikes have contributed to many a broken bone, but they've never broken my heart. I do tend to hide behind my racing – if things get tough or tricky in a relationship then I'll turn to racing and focus on that instead.

In recent years, I've playfully talked about myself as the

'grandmother of motorbike racing'. There are times when I look around the paddock and can't believe some of the riders are old enough to hold a licence, or even to shave. But I intend to race for as long as I'm able to get myself onto my bike, and so I'm sorry, Mum and Dad – but no wedding day, no grandchildren. (Or at least not yet, perhaps we should never say never!)

You might say it hardly makes me qualified to discuss the best way to raise children, and I don't want to bang on about it. But the one bit of advice I'd like to pass on, based on my own experience of life, is that trying to ban children, especially teenagers, from doing anything that they have their heart set on will only have the opposite effect. If they're anything like me, it will fuel their determination to defy their parents and follow their chosen path.

My mum and dad, bless them, were vehemently opposed to my decision to race motorbikes from the moment they first heard about it – which was some time after I'd started planning for it. According to Mum, I was *not* going racing in her lifetime. "Just go and get yourself a nice little car!" was her response whenever I raised the subject.

Nowadays, I can look back and appreciate how her reaction was partly the product of a woman's natural maternal instinct, and partly because she'd already witnessed the consequences of my first nasty accident on a road bike. Indeed, I was only able to finance myself in the world of motorbike racing after receiving a big compensation cheque at age 17, following a crash that threw me off my first proper bike, a Yamaha TZR125, and into a wall. I was hospitalised with injuries including a broken pelvis, elbow and knee, as well as a couple of fractured ribs. By comparison to later crashes and injuries it would be no big deal, and I got a cheque for nearly £8,000 from the insurers of the car driver who caused the accident. It was the money that gave me the chance to go racing.

The collision happened in my home village of Spratton, to the north of Northampton, with my mum just a few hundred yards away. Fortunately, though she was walking down the road towards me, she wasn't close enough to witness the impact itself. But it must have been a shock to arrive at the scene as the ambulance crew were scraping me off the pavement. Once the initial shock had worn off and Northampton General Hospital was putting me back together, our conversation was dominated by her insistence that I was never getting on a motorbike again. To buy her silence I agreed, yet I was already scheming behind her back to do the exact opposite.

The accident happened less than a month after I'd passed my road motorcycle test and two months after my 17th birthday. But, even before getting the TZR125, I'd had some experience of riding on two wheels after buying a rather sad little moped, a red Honda Melody with a little top-box on the back. It had no street credibility and my image was not helped by my cheap helmet and complete lack of decent riding gear. But it had only set me back £300, it was dirt cheap to run – only a tenner to tax it – and it gave me the chance to get out and about. That's something you want more than almost anything else when you've been brought up in a small village.

I'd left school at the age of 16 and got my first fulltime job as a trainee veterinary nurse at Spinney Lodge veterinary hospital in Northampton. I had no means of transport but obviously needed to get to and from town and, because the bus service in my village was rubbish, dear old Dad would drive me in and often collect me.

But I didn't want to be reliant on anyone. I wanted the independence to come and go as I pleased, and it wasn't fair on my dad to be doing this journey twice a day on my behalf. He'd had a heart attack a year previously, he still wasn't back to where he was before and I didn't want him running around for me – willing as he was.

I was always close to Dad as a young girl, and preferred helping him do his 'manly' jobs than being stuck in the kitchen with Mum. In 1989, shortly before I sat my GCSE exams, he'd had a major heart attack, which was obviously devastating for us all. He was a fit and healthy man, not quite 50, who worked outdoors a lot of the time and was always on the go. I was at school when it happened – he'd felt a bit funny during the day and lost the feeling in one of his arms. He was sitting at the kitchen table, finding it difficult to breathe, when Mum got home and she took him to hospital in Northampton. It was there that he was told he'd had a heart attack. He got sent to a hospital in Oxford for a multiple bypass operation – the surgeons had to cut through his ribcage to get to his heart. I know how painful it's been when I've broken ribs coming off my bike, but to have them sawn through must be so much worse.

Before this he had been a very active man, but after the operation he had to rest. (Like me, he wasn't very good at being poorly.) This all happened around my 16th birthday and, because I'd been out with him so often, it was easy for me to take on some of his work. One job was looking after the gardens of a teacher who lived in a nearby village called Hollowell, which were amazing, almost as big as a football pitch. I mowed her lawn with a big-pull Mountfield petrol mower and tended to her borders and flower beds; I also marked out the football pitches in Spratton for a six-a-side competition and tended to hedges and kerbs.

I enjoyed the physical work and didn't mind getting myself muddy and sweaty. I'd never been 'girlie' because I'd never felt pretty enough to compete with other girls in that arena. That's what my sister did, but I was nothing like her. We have come closer together in that respect in recent years, but she's still all about makeup, hair, clothes and shoes, while I'd rather be in my scruffs.

Perhaps that's one of the attractions of biking. You put on your leathers and clothes don't matter. You put your helmet on and you don't need to worry about your makeup or hair.

* * *

I came off that moped a few times. With my friend Tracey Brown, who lived in Hollowell, I used to scoot backwards and forwards between the villages. I had a favourite uncle, Len, who owned a smallholding on the outskirts of Hollowell and at the bottom of it was a concrete road where we used to burn the moped up and down, just to see how fast we could go. There were gates at each end of the road and we'd leave it to the last possible moment before braking in front of them. Then I got it wrong and smashed into the gate – the bike didn't come out of it too badly and I had only a few bumps and scrapes, but the gate was a wreck. I was like, "Oh my God, what have I done?" Tracey, a great pal, said, "Just blame me, tell your uncle I did it!"

So that's what we did, bless her. Although perhaps I should

have taken that tumble as a warning of things to come – after all, most people would give up after the first crash, although that didn't cross my mind. Perhaps I'm a glutton for punishment.

I'd saved the money to buy the moped by looking after other people's pets. I had these little cards made and put them through every door in the village. I was 13 when I started, and I bought a shed and an aviary. Dad helped me lay a slab of concrete in the garden so I had foundations for the outbuildings, and I'd charge people to take in their pets when they went on holiday or couldn't care for them. It was mainly cats and dogs, but I'd look after anything that was given to me.

Mum and Dad were really good about all these creatures taking up space in their back garden. They were just as supportive when, after starting work at the vets, I'd bring home all sorts of stray or injured animals. I'd left school to work with animals because I loved them and the thought of any creature – big or small – being put down was something I could never come to terms with, unless it was absolutely necessary. People would hand their pets in to be 'put to sleep' because they'd been blinded or lost a leg, or even because they no longer wanted the hassle of looking after them, but I couldn't see any of these as reasons to kill them. So I set up my own little pet rescue service, taking home those facing a death sentence and doing what I could to make them comfortable in the garden.

More often than not, I didn't tell my parents when there was a new arrival. I'd just find a place for them by annexing a bit more of Dad's garden, and they never said anything about the three-legged dog, the blind cat or the neglected lamb that might trip them up when they went into the garden to hang out the washing, or get the lawnmower out. Though Mum did eventually put her foot down and tell me no more dogs, because it wasn't fair on the neighbours. (I'd often pass some of these animals on to Uncle Len to keep on his smallholding.)

It took me a while to save the money for the moped because, although I was getting a fair amount of business from the pet-care venture, it also cost quite a lot to keep the animals. Of course, when I did have the £300 there was an argument over whether it should be spent on a means of transport that my parents saw as inherently dangerous, but I got my own way.

That moped was an accident waiting to happen. Its days were numbered when Dave Blencoe, our village policeman, told my mum that mopeds were the most dangerous things on the road. If I was going to ride on two wheels, he said, I should get a motorbike. I liked the sound of that because I definitely wanted something that was bigger, faster and cooler. Dave also told me that car drivers had no respect for mopeds, and many of them thought they belonged not on the road itself but in the gutter – which was obviously the worst place for them, because you'd be hitting all the drains and potholes, risking a bump that could knock you out in front of passing cars.

He was proved right when, a short while later, I was thrown off the moped. This time I was on my way from Spratton to a village called Chapel Brampton. It was all country lanes and, at a blind corner, I lost control, skidding off towards a bus coming from the other direction. It was terrifying. I remember thinking, *Flipping hell, that was close! I could have been scooped up!* But I got back on and carried on in a state of shock. When I got to Chapel Brampton I rang Tracey's mum – I could confide in her in a way that I couldn't with my own parents – and she came out to me. But once again, I only had a few bumps and bruises.

I used to ride my moped to work every day, I'd thrash it but it was dead slow. Just before I'd get to the vets there was a small roundabout, and I'd only just manage to stop because the brakes were so shoddy. I'd walk into work and Ian Fitzgerald, my favourite vet, would say, "Did you manage to stop this morning?" "Can you tighten up my brakes again, please?" I'd reply.

My parents (Mum in particular) started nagging me to get a car, but that Christmas some friends of the family came to our house. They had a son, Phillip, who would hone around the country lanes with a group of bikers, and when the conversation turned to me they asked, "Why don't you get a motorbike like Phillip?"

It seemed like a great idea, not least because I'd noticed Phillip and his mates gathering to sit around and chat before accelerating off on their bikes in a flurry of noise, speed and fumes. I'd have liked nothing more than to hang out with them. So, without my parents' knowledge, I asked Phillip to help me look for a bike – although it was his dad, John, who eventually suggested the Yamaha. Once I'd made up my mind, it was a decision that was to change my life.

I set my heart on the Yahama TZR125 when I saw it in a bike shop in Kettering. I knew Mum and Dad would not be happy about it, but I kept pointing out what Dave had said about bikes being better than mopeds. I wasn't a confrontational teenager but I had a strong streak of independence that could quickly develop into defiance, and the more they said 'no' the more I told myself I was going to do it.

Perhaps some girls go home and say, "I want to ride a

motorbike," so that their parents buy them a car, but mine were never likely to be in that position. That meant I had more control over what I did, because I had to do almost everything for myself. That was how I saw my life. I didn't want my parents holding my hand, helping me out. It was down to me, and that attitude helped me make my way in the sport. If I'd sat back and waited for somebody to help me out, perhaps I'd still be sitting there now.

The bike was priced at £1,200 and, on 9 March 1991, Dad drove me to the bank to pick up the £200 down payment in cash. I hadn't told them the model I wanted, so when we met Mum at the shop so she could sign the hire purchase documents for me, she strolled over to the scooters and asked me which one I was buying. When I pointed out the TZR125, she said, "You're not having that!" and walked out. I went running after her and begged her to go back, coming up with all these different ways of selling the bike to her – I promised her I'd do my CBT [compulsory basic training], I'd be the safest rider in the history of motorbikes and I'd never ride it fast. Eventually she agreed, although she insisted I had to pass the tests.

I was quite shy as a girl and, although I was desperate to go riding with Phillip and his pals, I'd have spent the rest of my teenage years peering at their little group from behind the front-room curtains if they hadn't come knocking for me. Tina was a good friend of Phillip's sister, so she knew him fairly well. She'd tell me to just walk up to the guys and start chatting. That's what she would have done without a second thought, but we're chalk and cheese – I never had the confidence to push myself forward.

The problem was solved when Phillip and company said they had seen me out and about on the bike, and did I want to go out for a ride with them? Tina insists she had nothing to do with them coming to call for me, but I'm not so sure. Whatever, I was straight into my leathers and out the door, and my family saw far less of me from that day onwards.

With the help of the lads, I got the bike derestricted so it could do just over a ton, and we'd spend all evening riding about the country lanes around Spratton. I'd come home from work, have my tea and head straight out. Mum and Dad wouldn't see me until the next morning, as by the time I'd get back they'd be in bed.

All the lads had their bikes derestricted to increase their power and enable them to accelerate quicker – it was all about getting the most out of the machines. Being teenagers, you pushed yourself to go faster and faster – until, of course, I ended up in hospital; although that accident had little to do with speed and plenty to do with the failing eyesight of the pensioner who pulled out on me in his car.

The lads came to the hospital to visit me every day. When my mum was sitting beside my bed they'd all be telling her, "No, Eileen, she's not getting a bike again," but as soon as she was gone they'd get out all their bike magazines and ask me what I was going to buy with my compensation money. Initially, the insurers offered just a few hundred pounds, but Phillip's dad got involved again and helped make sure I got what I was entitled to. Although it took me a few months to get the cheque, the £8,000 I finally received felt like a lottery win.

I only had that TZR125 for six months. After the crash I sold it; it was a bit scuffed up, but it definitely came out of it better than I did. Phillip wanted to buy it off me on the cheap, but I said no and sold it myself.

CHAPTER 2

HANGING OUT WITH THE LADS

I enjoyed my job at the veterinary hospital, but the training I received on day-release at colleges in Coventry and Birmingham was not what I needed – the lecturers specialised in human biology and didn't seem to have much of a clue as to how to apply it to animals. I guess the colleges just wanted to make some money, and those in charge thought that treating a cat or dog was not so different to treating a human being.

So I left Spinney Lodge and, despite still suffering the consequences of my crash, applied to go to a specialist college at Wood Green Animal Shelters in Cambridgeshire, which meant moving to St Ives. They provided the accommodation and I got put up with another girl on the same course, Nicki Bush, who saw me limp in on crutches and greeted me with, "Great, I get the cripple!"

We quickly became best mates and got up to all sorts of mischief at college and in our digs. We would always be laughing and, shortly after I had finally been able to stop using my crutches to walk, she had me in such a fit of the giggles that I lost my footing and fell down the stairs. I remember her standing over me in hysterics – thankfully, I did not do any further damage to the pelvis.

We would muck around together in class, although once it backfired when she threw what she thought was water at me – it was actually a strong alkaline solution that started to melt my face. As I panicked, she told our classmates that I was fooling around; I had to convince them I was genuinely in pain. I was taken to hospital, where a now mortified Nicki spent our entire time in Accident & Emergency apologising.

With the injuries from that crash taking their time to heal, I took up cycling in a bid to rebuild the strength of my legs. Mum's nagging had also left its mark, so I began to seriously consider whether I ought to get a car. One by one, the lads I'd been knocking about with also had their accidents; Phillip smashed up his 250, and that was the end of that; then another lad, Robert Lee, had a nasty crash on a bumpy road coming out of Spratton. A couple more lads ended up writing off their bikes and, by the time I headed back home after my nine-month stint in Cambridgeshire, most had traded what was left of their bikes for cars.

The pressure from my peers and parents to do the same was relentless, so I caved in and got a little banger of a Fiesta which didn't cost anywhere near as much as the bike. I've never had much luck with cars, and soon saw the end of this one. When I pulled into a petrol station and noticed smoke pouring out of the bonnet as I got out, the cashier screamed over the tannoy, "Turn your engine off now!" "I have!" I shouted back, waving the keys for her to see, as she shouted at me to get the car away from the pumps as quickly as possible.

With the Fiesta burnt out, I got a Golf, but that too was a disaster. The bonnet catch broke pretty much as soon as I bought it and I asked my dad if he could sort it out for me. Dad was always very good with his hands, and when he told me he'd fixed it I thanked him and went outside to have a look. I couldn't believe it – he'd drilled a couple of holes through the bonnet and run a piece of wire through them. It looked absolutely awful. I could have killed him – that was the last time I asked Dad to fix my car.

Even before I bought the TZR125, Mum and Dad had talked me into learning to drive a car. I was rushed into my first test when I wasn't ready – I even had to break the speed limit to get to the test centre on time. It was no problem for my instructor, as he regularly used to let me speed when he thought it was okay to do so. (I think you should be able to control a car at speed, or is that my love of high velocity talking?)

But getting to the centre on time didn't do me much good, as I failed. I re-took the test a short while later and failed again, so I decided it was time to go back to two wheels – which was much more fun anyway.

My parents kept on at me, however, so I took the driving test again and passed it in the same month that I passed part two of my bike test. Although the tests complement each other by making you more aware of other road users, all I really wanted to do was ride a motorbike and hang out with the lads in my village. It wouldn't be long before our little group all began to go their own way, but that spell buzzing the lanes with them was pretty much the coolest thing I'd done.

It was also these lads who took me to my first bike Grand Prix, at Donington Park, about 50 miles up the M1 from Spratton. I'd developed a typical teenage-girl fixation with biking legend Steve Hislop, who won the Isle of Man Tourist Trophy 11 times from 1984-94. It wasn't so much that he was handsome or dashing, although I thought he was, but that he was *the* main man in road racing at the time, and there was no need to put him on a pedestal because he was already up there.

I went on about him so much that a girl friend of mine, Hilary McEwan, took to drawing cartoons that took the mickey; just the normal schoolgirl sort of stuff about how Maria loved Steve, but they made me laugh and I've kept them to this day. At Donington, we stood at Coppice corner and Steve, who had been given a wildcard ride, came off his bike right in front of us. Although he got up okay, the lads ripped into him and I could have killed them. I'd so wanted him to do well that day, when I was watching all starry-eyed.

I often used to ride into Northampton with the guys, to hang around a junkyard bike shop called Davron's. Although my TZR125 had been repaired following its crash, I'd decided to get a bigger bike and used a bit more of my compensation money to upgrade to a Yamaha TZR250, which I used to get to work and back. I also bought a second-hand FZR600 Genesis which I sold a short while later for a profit. Next up was a Suzuki RGV250 which I used to race around the lanes with the guys.

I took a job in Market Harborough with Fox, White & Cleaver, where the vets all drove BMWs. Although I'd ride to and from work – a round trip of around 30 miles – on my

TZR250, whenever we'd go out on a visit they'd ask me if I wanted to drive their flash cars. They all pestered me to trade my bike in for a nice car, but there were two reasons why that line of persuasion was doomed: I was only taking home £370 a month, which was never going to buy me a BMW, and motorbikes had become more than ever the love of my life – in fact they'd become a way of life. The only time I questioned my decision was during the winter of 1993-4, when I had to ride to work in the snow and invariably ended up skidding off. I'd limp into the practice with bruised knees and spend the day hobbling around.

I'd got the job at Fox, White & Cleaver through a veterinary nurse, Carol, who I'd worked with at Spinney Lodge. My life had become all about animals and motorbikes, but I was beginning to have serious doubts about a career in the veterinary world. I couldn't stop thinking about bikes. After a visit to Brands Hatch to watch a race meeting I went out for a ride with a local bike group, the Sreknaws, and, according to my diary, it was one of the best times of my life so far; I then spent an afternoon as a sidecar passenger in a charity ride around Mallory Park. I was spending more and more time at Davron's, and never felt out of place among men of all ages, shapes and sizes who shared our common interest. I would often spend the weekend there, chatting about anything and everything with the guys.

As my enthusiasm for motorbikes grew, so I became disillusioned at the vets'. I'd passed my exams, qualified as a veterinary nurse (with distinction) and attended a passing-out ceremony in London with Mum, but I was still basically cleaning out crap and mopping up blood. I began to ask myself what all the hard work at college had been about, what was the point of learning all that stuff about anatomy and physiology when I wasn't putting much of it into practice?

There was a great vet there called Martin Cleaver and I loved working with him, but I was fed up with working with farmers and seeing at firsthand the nasty things they do to animals. I particularly hated working with the breeders, who were using animals to make money – and it was clearly only the money that mattered. They didn't care that they were putting bitches through one caesarean section after another, so long as they were getting loads of puppies out of them. Because they wanted big puppies they'd breed a bitch with a big dog, so they were never going to give birth naturally. They'd have so many sets of puppies that their bodies couldn't cope and they'd have to be cut open each time. It really started to play on my mind.

There were occasions when I'd assist in operations on farm horses or birds of prey, and I castrated a few cats. But for someone who became a veterinary nurse because she loved animals, the job wasn't working out as I'd hoped. The poor pay was always going to be an issue too, especially as I was becoming more independent and had started to think about leaving home.

With this and the joy of hanging out at Davron's in mind, I walked into Midland Motorcycles in Northampton, where I also used to hang out regularly, and asked if there were any jobs going. It was only on the spur of the moment, but a guy in the parts department told me they were looking for an assistant in sales. So I went down to see a man called Sid, who looked 100 years old but was probably not much more than half that. His appearance wasn't helped by his white hair being tinged yellow by relentless smoking. The walls of his office were supposedly white, but they were also stained yellow by the inescapable nicotine.

Not that I cared too much, because he interviewed me on the spot and offered me the job.

And so Maria Costello, the veterinary nurse, became Maria Costello the motorcycle sales assistant. I felt at home from the first day and I loved it there. It was a good time for biking, which was a thriving industry in the early 1990s. Midland Motorcycles was a big dealership, despite the building being a bit tatty and old school. It was also warm and friendly, a really sociable place where people would come in at weekends to hang out.

CHAPTER 3

I WANT TO RACE!

Hanging out at Davron's and working at Midland Motorcycles meant listening to countless tales of track bravado from the bikers who spent their time there. They made their exploits sound so exciting: their accidents and injuries were a badge of honour, even their lengthy spells in hospital were made to sound like an adventure.

Of course, bikers are going to make light of their injuries – you'd not be much of a racer if you set off worrying about getting hurt. Some never bothered speaking about their mishaps, but there were others who seemed to delight in passing on all the gory details. But then, if you smash up your shoulder, knee or ribs, or scrape the skin off of your arm or leg, and go through all the recovery only to get back on a bike, knowing you might well go through it all again, you're entitled to talk yourself up a bit.

It was very much a 'boy's own' club. Although I can't say I was ever a tomboy, I was never a 'girlie girl' either. I was more comfortable in that environment than I was shopping for clothes or makeup, or spending hours at the hairdressers. After listening to the tales of the track, paddock and pit-lane, there was no way that at closing time I could just get on my bike, go home and forget about it all. Indeed, most days I rode home replaying some of the more memorable conversations in my head.

I've always been good with money – I've never had much, so I've needed to be – and I'd invested the compensation I received from the elderly driver with the dodgy eyes' insurance. But it was beginning to burn a hole in my pocket. The urge to spend at least some of it on what I needed to take my next step towards becoming a racer was growing stronger. Knowing what my parents would say, I dillied and dallied until the day I popped back up to my old school, Guilsborough, to see some mates who'd stayed on to do their A-levels. I turned up on my RGV250 but still had the same cheap Centurion helmet that I'd bought with my Honda Melody – you could even see the join in it. One of the lads went, "You've got a great motorbike, but look at your crap helmet!"

That was it. I didn't want anyone talking to me like that and anyway, I wanted to look the part when I was hanging out at Davron's and Midlands Motorcycles. I vowed to treat myself, so I bought the Arai helmet I'd long dreamed of – these were the best helmets on the market according to all the bike magazines – from Midlands Motorcycles, and then went with a friend to a bike clothing shop in Leicester to buy a particular brand of leathers I'd decided I must have. I spent a lot of money on Dainese one-piece leathers and gloves, as well as

Alpine Star boots. I've still got all that stuff – the leathers and gloves set me back over a grand, while I paid somewhere between £150 to £200 for the boots, which I bought simply because they were the same ones as those worn by Steve Hislop, in white and red. At the time they were what all the racers were wearing, although I was later to find that they didn't give you quite as much protection as you might hope. I didn't spare a penny that day, and among the other stuff I bought was a back protector. At this stage it was more about looking the part than *being* it, and I guess I looked like a real spoiled brat.

The must-read magazine of the time was *Performance Bikes* and Kev Smith, who road-tested for it, would come into Midland Motorcycles to visit a mate who worked there. He could rear-wheel steer, which is something few bikers can manage successfully, and I had a crush on him. Whenever he walked in, I'd go, "Ah, Kev ..."

Again, I was too shy to do anything more than look at him. Despite going to a mixed school, I'd never had a boyfriend. I had short dark hair, I wore very little makeup, I didn't feel I was pretty or cool, so therefore I was never going to get a boyfriend, was I? I didn't have enough confidence in myself to think that a boy might fancy me. Once, when I was with a group of friends who were trying on lipstick – we were only 12 or 13 years old – I took my turn and they all burst out laughing at me. I felt so ugly and walked away thinking, "I can't even wear lipstick ..." It's terrible how such little things have such a big impact on you, giving your self-doubt something to latch onto and making it so much harder to see yourself for what you really are. I'd always been a bit of a joker when I was young and I think that was my way of coping, trying to make up for the fact that I didn't think there was anything attractive about me.

Years later, I'd end up working with Kev at *Performance Bikes* on road tests together – although by then the crush had gone. Indeed, many of the guys who were my idols in my teenage years have gone on to become my mates.

I stayed with Midland Motorcycles for two years, but then came an opportunity that was to lead me not only to a new job but also to the chance to race. I'd been regularly going to watch racing at Donington, Mallory and Brands Hatch; I'd spoken with a couple of mates, Neil Townley and Nick Moss-Norbury, about possibly sharing a bike to go racing and they seemed up for it, but they both had girlfriends and that limited their time to go racing.

Although I had the desire and the gear, it took me a while to build enough confidence to go racing. But then I got a job with RGS Motorsport in Wellingborough, which was a performance-car garage owned by Gary Ward, who raced cars and was a decent bloke. His plan was to start selling bike parts to complement his car business, and so I joined him to help get it going. He kept telling me to follow my dream, talked to me endlessly about race craft and even sorted out a place for me to store my bikes, in a unit next to his. When I wasn't working, I almost lived in that little unit. I even moved out of my parents' home to lodge with one of the guys who worked for Gary, because it was close to the unit.

One of the bikers I'd got to know was a guy called Dave Weston, who I'd met through our mutual mate Neil Townley and who was already a racer. Neil, Nick and I had talked about going racing and Dave said he'd help us, although nothing came of it. However, when I moved to Wellingborough I would often pop round to see Dave, who lived with his wife Caroline in the town. In my early days as a racer I definitely looked upon him as my mentor, and I'd go round to their house just to talk about motorbikes. It could have driven Caroline mad, but she was always lovely to me and welcomed me into their home.

There were many times when I stayed in my little unit until gone midnight, and Dave would sometimes give me a hand. He taught me the basics of mechanics, things like how to change the reed valves. He also got me to ease off with all the chemicals I'd bought to clean and service the bike, because I used so many that if you shut the door you'd get high; combined with the fuel which I spilled on the floor, it wasn't the safest environment in which to spend hours on end. Fortunately, I've never smoked ...

While I was living in Wellingborough I had another real banger of a car, a crappy old Fiesta. It looked so out of place in the RGS car-park next to the boss's Ford Escort Cosworth and the souped-up little sporty things that lots of the young lads drove. There's a loop around Wellingborough town centre that these lads would buzz around, and sometimes I'd race them on my way home. My Fiesta was an embarrassment, it wasn't hard to get it sliding, and they wouldn't want to be seen with me, but it always made me laugh to see their faces if I pulled alongside them. I was beginning to develop a competitive instinct – and also to discover that for some men, at least, there seemed to be nothing worse than being beaten for speed by a girl

I still held back from throwing myself into racing, I guess the self-doubt that has been with me all my life wasn't that easy to overcome. Then I went to a track day at Mallory Park with some mates, and spent the day riding around on my road bike with an instructor. I had a big slide at the Esses, a notorious S-shaped bend, but got it back and the instructor said to me, "That was very good, very good riding, have you thought about racing?"

Wow! That was what I needed to hear. His words were a green light. I rode home that day telling myself, *He said I can go racing, so I'm going to go racing!* As soon as I got back to Wellingborough I called Dave up and said, "I'm going racing, can you help me find a bike?"

Not for the first or last time, Dave went out of his way to help. He started making calls and quickly came up with something he thought would interest me. He'd raced with this guy who had a Suzuki RGV250 for sale, which grabbed me because I already had one of these on the road and it was just awesome. We went down south to have a look at it, finding it tuned and ready for racing. It was the one for me – money permitting. This lad was from quite an affluent family, so he threw in loads of spares to make it pretty much the complete package for £3,400.

The bike's engine had been tweaked a little and, because it

had already been run, it was ready for me to take it away and race it. Dave had a proper race bike that he was forever taking apart – taking the head off, replacing the pistons, plug chopping, there was always something to do. But my bike was a lot easier than Dave's to maintain, all I had to do was fuel up, change the gearing from circuit to circuit and set tyre pressures. One thing I did change immediately was the pink paint scheme, which obviously had to go – pink has never really been my colour.

As a young girl I'd spent many weekends at my Uncle Len's smallholding, and he had no problem letting me use his spanners, screwdrivers, drills and any other tool to hand. Without making a big deal about it he made me believe I could work with tools, so I grew up thinking there was no reason why I shouldn't. He was always tinkering with something or other and got me driving his diggers or tractors, as well as showing me the basics of welding. It gave me a can-do attitude, at least as far as working with my hands is concerned, and it's probably why I enjoyed working on my bikes so much.

When I got stuck I had Dave to help me out, although he encouraged me to work independently whenever possible. He'd stand over me saying, "You strip it down," "You take the fairings off," "You take the wheels off," "You change the sprockets," and then he'd get to work on the engine. When it needed new pistons he'd be around to put those in, while he showed me how to set up the re-valves and the power valves. He never seemed to lose his cool and, although I never took it for granted, I didn't really appreciate at the time quite how much knowledge he was passing on.

Getting the bike ready was one thing, finding the money to race it was something else. Even the basic costs of racing a bike – entry fees, transport, fuel, tyres – can be prohibitive, and I've known guys who have spent almost every penny they've ever earned on their racing. If you want to ride at a competent level you've got to find a five-figure sum each year, which for many people is just not going to happen.

Although I'd been shy as a youngster, I'd also inherited some of my mum's cheek. She's never been afraid to speak out or ask for help, and as I reached my twenties I began to feel more confident about going to people. I guess my jobs at Midland Motorcycles and RGS had forced me to open up a bit more, and after putting in all that work on getting the bike into the best condition possible the desire to race it dominated everything. I knew, if I was going to give myself a chance, I'd have to sell myself to potential backers. *This is what you've chosen to do – now go out and do it,* I started to tell myself.

I'd made some good contacts in the motorcycle world and I went to them first. This is where being female did provide an unexpected advantage. I hadn't even raced, yet there were people who were prepared to back me; in most cases it was just a bit of kit, a few accessories or some spares, but it was more than many of the guys who'd been racing for years were getting. There were hundreds of them battling for sponsorship, but because I was a young, blonde (courtesy of a bottle), reasonably presentable woman, I guess they looked at me and thought there might be a bit of publicity in it for them. I even persuaded Budget to give me a van to take the bike to meetings, which was obviously a big deal for me.

Gary was also a great help. Apart from tapping up his own contacts he encouraged me to write letters and spent a lot of time showing me the right way to approach people. I went at it with great enthusiasm and, despite having no form, suddenly found I had companies in the trade saying, "Yeah, we'll help you by giving you parts," or by doing my paintwork. Even a local insurance company gave me a few hundred quid. I took whatever I could get, and Gary found me sponsors who were happy to pay my entry fees or buy the odd set of tyres.

It all seemed to come quite easily; it certainly didn't seem like a battle, yet I was aware I had little to offer in return. I guess they thought there was enough of a novelty factor about a female bike racer (even though I wouldn't be the only one) to interest the media and give them a bit of exposure. Being as innocent as I was and barely into my twenties, I also had my first experience of being taken for a ride.

One local businessman, Dominic Companero, approached me after reading a local newspaper article about me and offered to buy me everything I needed to race. He seemed genuine enough and, after meeting with him and chatting some more, it got to the point where I got Dave Weston involved and went off to start looking at race bikes. I was like, "Wow, I've got this amazing sponsor!" and Dave was like, "Just be a little careful, Maria, until you see what this guy is up to." Dave was right, because this guy vanished off the face of the earth. I don't know what happened, whether he went bankrupt and fled the country or whatever, but one day we were talking about how much he was going to give me and the next day he was gone. I never heard from him again. He was involved with a pub not too far from me so I rode over there, but he was nowhere to be seen. It was a surreal experience, at times it almost felt like I'd dreamed the whole thing up. But I hadn't.

So I continued my search for backing and started contacting the local media to generate some interest. I'd already started to build up a few local contacts, having written reports on the Northamptonshire SchoolBoy Motorcross Club for the local papers and motorbike press. I'm the first to admit that my grammar, spelling and punctuation are often not what they should be, but it gave me an insight into getting yourself in the press. I made a point of not just writing up the results but trying to compose a story. I'd also try to include stuff on the kids who were not at the front but still had a story to tell. If I missed anybody out then, at the next meeting, I'd either have some demented dad screaming at me or a sulky dad not speaking to me.

Many of these men seemed to be living their biker dream through their kids, who they'd be terrorising at the back of the circuit. They'd be slapping them on the back of the head, yelling at them to go for it, telling them not to accept finishing second, that there were no excuses for not winning. So many kids nowadays are not left to make their own way in sport, there always seems to be somebody shouting at them or giving them a hard time. I've seen how destructive this competitive dad mentality can be – half the kids give up as soon as they can because what they're going through is anything but enjoyable. Then they'll hide away in their bedroom on their PlayStation or X-box.

Having followed Dave around as he raced, I'd learned a bit about race meetings. I was only on the fringes but I loved everything about them. He was racing 250s at the time and, one Wednesday, I went with him to Mallory Park, where they let cars tear around the track in the morning and motorcycles in the afternoon. You paid your £40 and took your turn around the circuit, but I was hesitant and crashed on my first lap. My initial instinct was to dissolve into tears, but I made a real point of not doing so, telling myself, *Don't you dare cry, you're a biker now, be tough!* I wasn't hurt, but I was really embarrassed because I knew people would have seen the crash and thought, "Silly girl, who does she think she is, riding a race bike?" So I bit my lip, got up, got back on the bike and continued.

If my parents had been set against me riding a road bike, that was nothing compared to their dismay when I plucked up the courage to tell them I was going racing. They really flipped, and we had row after barnstorming row as they tried to stop me doing something they felt was far too dangerous for their daughter. But my decision to compete hadn't been an overnight one; it had taken me many months to overcome my doubts and, once I'd made up my mind, nothing was going to stop me.

They tried every tactic in the book of parenting to talk me out of it, but they weren't getting anywhere. I began to feel I didn't want to be around them. I'd tell myself that Mum didn't want me riding a *horse*, for heaven's sake, let alone a motorbike, so if they were going to be so horrible then I'd just have to go off and make my own way in the sport.

CHAPTER 4

MY FIRST RACE

My first race was at Mallory Park in the spring of 1995. The season was already underway and early on I'd gone with Dave to watch him race at the same venue, where Sandra Barnett was also competing. Sandra was one of a handful of women racers, and was married to TT rider Pete Barnett. As with another female racer, Kate Parkinson, she'd raced in the Manx Grand Prix before turning to the TT; with both of them racing well, 1995 could have been the year when women finally started to make a bit of headway.

Sandra was the only woman competing at Mallory Park that day. I sat in the back of Dave's van with him, as it was raining, and was probably driving him up the wall with my non-stop chatter about all my big plans. If only I could find the courage to put them into place! As the rain began to clear, and we watched Sandra go into the pit-lane, Dave turned to me and said, "See, girls can race." I thought to myself, *If she can do it, so can I ...*

And so I finally plucked up the courage to fill in my entry

form for a club meeting. At the time, I thought it was pretty much the bravest thing I'd ever done.

With my fairings – the shell which fits over the bike frame – having been sent away for a paint job, to get rid of the dreaded pink, I turned up at Mallory Park with a version in plain yellow. I guess it was the only paint spray I had at the time, but it made me feel slightly less conspicuous.

Dave, Nick and Neil were all there to support me. I'd thought about not telling my family on the basis of what they didn't know couldn't hurt them (and could save me from another lecture), but a couple of days before the event I walked into my parents' front room and said, "I'm racing this weekend but don't think you're coming, I don't want you there." My sister, Tina, said to me, "What are you wasting your money for – why don't you just buy yourself some nice clothes?" She had no idea what it was that I wanted. I adopted a confrontational tone with all three of them, ready for a fight, I guess because I didn't want to show any weaknesses that they could exploit.

Some parts of the first race day I remember very clearly, but too much is a blur. I had packed my Budget van the night before and then, only able to sleep fitfully, got up far too early. I followed Dave and, when we got to the paddock, set up next to him. He set up his awning so he could work under cover but I didn't have any, so I worked out of the back of my van. Mostly I was just copying what he did. It was Dave who saw me through the different stages of preparation, leading me around to get signed in, getting the bike scrutineered to basically ensure it will not fall to pieces or hurt anyone and the race numbers on, even telling me when to put my leathers on!

It was raining that day, and it did cross my mind that maybe I shouldn't go out. But then I told myself I was there to race, and I was going to do it. I was full of contradictions. I looked through the fence at the side of the track as one race got underway and thought to myself, *Oh, my God, I've got to do that in a minute!* I'd watched Dave enough times, but I really wasn't prepared for what was happening to me. My nerves were shot, I was close to panic and, although I really *did* want to race, I needed someone strong to get me focused and calm.

A lot of people go into racing because it's in the family, so they've got a dad or an uncle to support them. I had made a point of shutting my family out, so Dave was the one I was most reliant on. But it meant he had to deal with someone who was all over the place. I started fretting that I hadn't practised a start and began to flip. But Dave was his normal cool self and told me, "You'll be fine – just set off when the flag drops."

Dave had to go off, so I turned to Neil and said, "What do I do?" He said I should rev the bike really high and just dump the clutch. He was the last person I spoke to before the start, which was a big mistake because I revved it as high as I could, dumped the clutch and did a massive wheelie – but the bike didn't move! It was a standstill wheelie, it just went *bang!* – straight up. I know that somebody, somewhere, has got that on video, because I've seen it – all you see is this little yellow bike going up and everybody else scooting off into the first corner.

er, it didn't turn out too badly because there were 0 bikers and a lot of bunching up and fairing bashing at that first corner. I missed all that, but got going and caught the tail-enders up, tagging onto them before overtaking a couple. I definitely felt my confidence grow as the race progressed, although the overdose of adrenaline has blotted out my finishing position. But it definitely wasn't last.

I got such a kick from that race – the buzz was out of this world, and I headed off with a real sense of achievement. All the doubts, the indecision, the worries over what my family would say were in the past. There would be no going back; this was the life for me.

I sent in my report to the local paper and they hooked onto it straight away. I really didn't want to make a fuss about being a girl, but the *Northampton Chronicle & Echo* immediately seized on the angle of the 'biker chick' – which I hated, although it did prove a help when it came to seeking backers. I soon got used to being called 'biker chick' or 'biker babe', which obviously fitted well into headlines and made the sub-editor's job a bit easier!

I was hardly an overnight success though. Dave insisted that I should ride in as many races as I could; although I'd always be towards the back, his plan was to get me as much track time as he could. You might think you can ride a motorbike because you've honed around country lanes on a derestricted road machine, but don't kid yourself. Dave would encourage me to go out in the Formula 400 class and then I'd go out in the 250 race. Although my bike was a 250 it was a production bike, whereas Dave and most other people on the grid were on proper Grand Prix machines. So I'd go out and not do so well, but I had to keep telling myself it was a learning process.

Because my parents continued to show no desire to back me and racing had become a taboo subject in the Costello family home, I'd begun to distance myself from them. After returning home from one race where I had a minor tumble but was unhurt, I shouted at them that they were banned from ever watching me race – it was a hollow threat because it seemed that was the last thing they were ever going to do, but I was quite prepared to go it alone.

And, with each outing, I showed improvement as my race technique and confidence grew. I got a second and third place in my eighth and ninth races and then won my tenth novice race from the back of the grid. The feeling as I saw the chequered flag was amazing, and for one of the first times in my life I actually felt I was pretty cool.

If I struggle to remember my debut race, I can pretty much tell you everything from start to finish about winning that one. I worked my way through the field to the front and then this guy overtook me. We kept going at each other and I overtook him before he went past me again to lead. I think he thought he'd got the race, but I caught up with him just on the line.

I was only presented with a little cup, but I felt like Steve Hislop. Despite my determination to be a tough biker, I had a little cry. I felt really pleased with myself as I walked back to my van, and perhaps the guy I'd just beaten felt I was smiling a bit too much. He was parked opposite me, so I called out, "Well done, good race!" But he wouldn't answer. He turned his back and I remember thinking, *He's all grumpy because he got beaten by a girl – how awful was that for him?*

I put the cup on the dashboard of my van and drove straight round to my parents. Mum said, "Yes, very good," and started talking about the weather or something. It had been me who had shut them out, after all. But still, I felt, *I've got to do something better than this to get their attention.*

I didn't tell them about all the mishaps I had in those first races. I crashed several times without hurting myself other than a few scuffs and bruises, but I used up all my spare parts pretty quickly. You'd have to be pretty unique to come into racing as a novice and not go through that process, and to me it was just part of learning my race craft. Only then could I get to know the limit of my tyres or how far I could lean the bike over. In one race, a guy swooped down towards me and I thought, *He's going to hit me*, so I touched my front brake and that was it – I lost my grip, my front went and I low-sided the bike. I wasn't hurt, I just scraped the bike, but, as Dave told me as he helped load the bike into the van, you have to accept the spills because they're part of the process of finding your boundaries.

It wasn't as if I hadn't had plenty of spills already. Apart from my moped and road bike crashes, I'd gone horse-riding as a girl and fell off loads of times. I'm a mountain bike enthusiast as well and have come off that enough times, so perhaps I've just got crappy balance. Anyway, on a motorbike you have all your kit on and it's your leathers that should take the brunt of the crash – that's the whole point of spending all that money on protection.

It's not something you can allow to play on your mind. If you did you'd never get back on a bike, because the one thing you can guarantee is that if you're racing to avoid having a crash then you're nailed on to have one. I've never felt I'm indestructible, but in my first year I had enough spills to learn that you can often manage them to minimise their impact. Of course, there will always be exceptions, but that's something you don't dwell on. How could you race if you did?

Besides, I was enjoying myself too much to worry. I was getting a thrill from pushing myself against other bikers and going as fast as I could. I'd always had a thing about speed, and when I was going through my horse-riding phase I'd sneak on the gallops at Teeton, which was later to be home to the National Hunt legend Teeton Mill, and push my little pony as fast as it would go. It was never fast enough, and in that first season I felt the same about my racing. Race bikes don't have a speedometer, only a rev counter, but I knew I was going at more than 100mph, hitting top speeds of around 140. But all I wanted was to go faster.

Dave was a bit of a Mallory Park specialist, but that year he came to lots of other tracks with me. We went to Caldwell, Snetterton and Brands Hatch, and I was getting a bit of attention in the paddock – heads would turn as this blonde ponytail bobbed by – and I had a few guys come up to offer to help. Dave had his own calendar and commitments so he couldn't always be there for me. So when this guy who'd been friendly to me offered his support, I said yes – unfortunately, although his heart was in the right place, he wasn't the best mechanic. But once again, it was a learning experience; anyone in sport will tell you how you'll come across people who talk a big game but fail to deliver. He said he'd be my mechanic at one particular race at Cadwell, but we were late getting there because he got us lost, the chain came off the bike and then I ran out of fuel and had to push the bike back to the paddock, and that hill at Cadwell is flipping steep! He kept saying that all he wanted to do was go racing. He reckoned he knew it all and kept telling me things like, "You should have done better there," or, "You didn't do very well there," but it quickly dawned on me that this guy actually had no idea. He would go on and on, "I want to go racing, I want to go racing" – so finally I turned round and said, "Well, go racing then."

He went off to do his own thing and I wasn't too sad to see him go. Then, a short while later, I organised a track day at Mallory Park for Midland Motorcycles. It was a really good day, the weather was great, and then this same guy came along with a race bike he'd bought. He went out on the track and I couldn't let a chance like that go by, so I jumped on a 125 from Aprilia, who were there offering track test rides, and said to myself, "I'm going to show him!" I was one of the least competitive people you could meet when I was at school, yet there was something about motorbikes that brought out the monster in me. I flew past him so close I almost licked his paint, before coming in and telling him, "You should have done better there." He just glared at me, so I laughed and said, "Now tell me to go faster."

Apart from the odd one, I've had good people around me when I've gone racing, some of whom have since become very good friends. Then, towards the end of that first season, I went to Mallory Park for a club meeting. I was putting a sprocket on the wheel ahead of my race when my mate Steve, who was helping me with the bike, tapped me on the shoulder and said, "Your mum and dad are here." I looked up and saw them, and I nearly started crying. Only then did I realise what a big thing it was to have them support me. They hadn't changed their opinion – I know where I get my stubbornness from – but they'd decided that if I was going to race then, regardless of their genuine concerns, they would have to be there for me. They didn't say a lot, but Dad watched me work on the bike and said to Steve, "I didn't know she could use spanners." Mum said she couldn't watch me race and went back to sit in the car.

Dad started coming along to the odd meeting with one of my uncles, and he got to know Dave Weston. It was obvious he liked him and when we'd get home all Dad would talk about was Dave. I would sit there thinking, *When is he going to talk about me?* Then, one day, Mum told me that he couldn't tell me to my face, but my dad was very proud of me – something he was apparently quite happy to tell other people.

Mum is still not keen on coming to races because, I guess, she fears the worst. I can understand that. I'm sure that, if I had a daughter, I'd want to wrap her in cotton wool.

It took a long time to win them round, but once they

accepted me as a racer they started gathering quite a collection of newspaper and magazine cuttings, photographs and videotapes of whenever I appeared on television. They've got to know the names of all the racers I've competed against and the bikes I've raced, and kept a record of my results. I know they dread the phone ringing when I'm away at a meeting, and I try to protect them by telling my helpers that, whatever happens, *nobody* is ever to ring them.

CHAPTER 5

ONE FOR THE GIRLS!

In that first year of racing, I was determined not to let anybody put me down because I was a woman. But there's no getting away from the fact that, of the 7,000-plus qualified bike racers in the UK, over 97 per cent are men. Women racers *are* a novelty, and even though I'd try hard to feel at home in the paddock I got plenty of funny looks from a lot of guys. Some of them would stop what they were doing and just gawp when I'd walk through, but, despite not always being as confident as I tried to portray myself, I did have some attitude. When a guy stared too long or too hard I would say to myself, *Yeah, I'm a girl and I'm going to beat you.* If things weren't going well or I was a bit wound-up, I might snap, "What are you looking at?" and they'd either smile or snarl and turn away.

I've been in the paddock for so long now that I know what's going to happen, and I've come to accept it. But in those early days I didn't want anybody staring at *me*, so I guess I hid behind my leathers and helmet a little. I'd been very self-conscious long before I got into racing, so it was impossible not to feel uncomfortable when I felt everyone was looking at me, and I started thinking that perhaps I should make more of an effort with my appearance.

I took a bit more time over my makeup and hair, but it was something I used to moan about. Dave Jefferies, the TT legend who was to become a great mate, said to me once, "Why do you bother? You don't have to do yourself up to race." He told me not to worry about what other people were thinking or saying, but when you're a female with low self-worth and suddenly you've got a bit of a public persona, it can be hard. As I became better known, I even stopped going to Tesco in my scruffs because I didn't want anybody to see me and think, "There goes Maria – can't be bothered to make the effort."

There is tremendous pressure on girls from a young age to conform to a certain image, and I did used to get caught up with what other people thought about me rather than just being myself. The relentless media focus on facial beauty and body shape destroys the confidence of so many women, and I was no different. I've spent much of my life feeling inadequate and insecure, and I've never had much self-esteem. Fortunately for me, biking has been an escape – once I'm on the start line I become Maria the bike racer, and I just get on with it. Everything else is left behind, at least until the walk back through the paddock.

Over the years I've toughened up, and there have been times when I've enjoyed the attention – although I'm still not comfortable with being *the* centre of attention. I've had to accept that, for as long as I race, I'm going to be seen as somehow different, a bit of an oddity, because for most people girls just don't race motorbikes.

For the past 15 years I've had people queuing up to tell me to pack it in, and I'm sure my dad still thinks that today. He was always saying to me, "Stop living in a dream world," but would he have said that to a boy? If I'd been born male, would people have told me to forget about racing and get a 'proper job'? If I was absolutely useless perhaps, but I was being told this even after I'd proven I could race a bit.

I hate being put in a box, yet it happens to so many girls. I'd spent a lot of my childhood working with my hands at my Uncle Len's farm and doing jobs for Dad, yet as soon as I showed an interest in motorbikes most people basically started telling me to get back to my makeup and hair extensions.

But why can't girls race? We let them go off to fight in the army nowadays, so surely we can be allowed to ride in a motorbike race without feeling we're doing something that's somehow forbidden?

And, of course, I wanted to beat the guys – that was what everybody was there to do. There's a lot of testosterone in the sport, and the way some of the guys would stride around the paddock as if they owned the place did wind me up. They seemed to puff out their chests when they saw me, and I'd think to myself, *Why are they doing that? I don't like that at all*. But I'd be the last person to go looking for confrontation.

There were times when it would get me down, I'd leave the paddock to go back to my van and my shoulders would slump – it could be quite tiresome being a one-woman sideshow. I did feel as if some of the guys were just waiting for me to fail, that some were actively willing it, and although I'd tell myself to ignore them or to use it as motivation, you'd have to be much tougher than I was for it not to get to you occasionally. All I really needed was to belong, but I was an outsider. I wanted to put my helmet on, to put my leathers on, to fit in and be everyone's friend.

Perhaps that really isn't all that healthy and says something about the woman I was. But there were times when I'd get philosophical and say to myself, *I'm doing the same as them but I'm being treated differently in every respect*. Sure, I could see why the guys wouldn't like being beaten by a girl, but my philosophy was that they shouldn't like being beaten by anybody. Why should losing to me be any worse than losing to a male rival?

Unfortunately, there wasn't a lot I could do about it. Female riders have always been few and far between in this sport – although the irony is that this is one of the few sports in which women can compete on pretty much equal terms. In athletics or football or rugby, for example, we'll never be truly equal because of the basic realities of physique and strength. But there's no reason why a woman can't do as well as a man in bike racing – you don't have to be built like Tarzan or have the muscles of Arnold Schwarzenegger. Indeed, most of the top riders are pretty scrawny with body shapes close to tri-athletes, because you don't want to bulk up – it's much more to do with total fitness involving suppleness and stamina rather than brute strength, and women have those physical attributes just as much as men.

Perhaps too many girls have parents like mine, who think the last place for a girl is on a motorbike. However, the number of women who own motorbikes in the UK has risen to around 125,000, so perhaps attitudes are beginning to change. I hope so, because there were too many times in that first season when I was made to feel I was an outsider. But I'd set my heart on racing and I wasn't going to pack up and go away; so I told myself that, whenever possible, I'd use the negativity in a positive way. I surprised myself by how strong I was in dealing with the negative vibes.

* * *

Being a female did have its advantage when, with less than a season's racing under my belt, I got approached to ride in my first team. Only this one was going to be a little bit different to the norm – the first all-female bike team in the UK!

The opportunity came out of the blue. I was packing the van after finishing a meeting at Mallory Park when Pete Barnett came over and started chatting. Pete's wife is Sandra Barnett, the woman rider who had helped convince me I could make a go of racing, even if she didn't know it. Pete said, "Would you be interested in riding in an all-girl team next year?" My mechanic overheard the conversation and was like, "This is amazing, you're being offered rides in your first year!" I told Pete that of course I'd be interested. His plan was to put together a trio of women to attract sponsors and he'd already started the ball rolling. He told me they'd be me, Sandra and a girl called Bridget McManus, and we'd all be on Honda CBR 600s, which would mean I'd race a four-stroke, a different category of racing, for the first time.

It was a clever bit of thinking by Pete, and attracted plenty of interest. We were something different and we got loads of publicity from the launch party, which was held at a hotel in Evesham where Sandra worked. I even let my mum and dad come along. We had a double-page spread in *Motorcycle News* to kick us off and plenty of other coverage, definitely more than an equivalent male team would have got. Sure, the top riders with a big professional team behind them would always get their share of the newspapers, magazines and TV, but we weren't anywhere near the best in the UK. However, we were girls in a man's world and that made for a news story. We were called the George Pilkington race team after the main sponsor, who made dentures; there's obviously a lot of money to be made from false teeth, because his support was good.

The team supplied all the bikes, while I had to cover some of the costs such as tyres, fuel and entry fees, which I was able to do with the help of my personal sponsors. I was excited at the prospect of using somebody else's race bike, especially as it meant I got to sell mine, although the money I received went straight back into racing.

I was told that we'd be concentrating on short circuits in our first year (1996), so that Bridget and I could get enough racing under our belts to qualify for our national licences, and once that was sorted we'd be going to the Isle of Man – a fantastic prospect! Pete said that Bridget and I would do the Manx Grand Prix, which comes toward the end of the season, with Sandra doing the TT.

It all seemed so positive, although in the back of my mind I had some nagging doubts. As an all-female team we were trading on our sex, and probably making it even harder to win the acceptance of the guys. It obviously wasn't such an issue for Sandra because she was married to a racer. She was also quite a bit older and more experienced than me, being the fastest woman at the Isle of Man. But while Bridget was closer to my age and had been riding for only around the same time as me, she had a really lovely boyfriend who did everything for her. I was the one who had to do pretty much everything herself.

I'd watched Sandra quite a lot in my first year and had a lot of respect for her as a racer, even if I didn't know her as a person. With her being the fastest woman around the TT, I had someone to emulate and felt I was making progress with every race. It wasn't only about how I handled the bike, but also picking up on what the others were up to, how races unfolded, when you took your chances and how the top guys implemented their race plan – course craft, in other words. It was a world completely new to a girl who only a short while previously had been a veterinary nurse from Northants.

The season started okay. All of the club racing was going alright; we were getting in the top ten places. We were causing a bit of a stir as the only all-woman team, getting what the men saw as a disproportionate amount of publicity. We worked hard for it, we had to go out and sell ourselves, yet it still felt like some of them didn't want us there. It was in the way they looked at us, shut us out of conversations or stopped talking when they saw one of us walking through the paddock. To them, the only women who fitted in were their wives or girlfriends – or their bits on the side; the pretty ones holding the brollies and massaging the men's egos. Not everyone was that way, but in motorcycle racing there are plenty of men who don't expect much more from a female than that she should look pretty.

I bet those guys never even contemplated that we might beat them. So when we did start overtaking a few of them they had to wake up and take note. Finishing behind a girl meant they'd take a load of stick off their mates, which was something they really wanted to avoid. It certainly didn't gain us any more acceptance, but I think we earned a bit of respect as the season progressed.

While the male riders were pretty much a closed shop – with a few notable exceptions – I felt even more isolated because I never got close to Sandra or Bridget. I respected Sandra enormously for her TT record, but she never became the mentor that she could have been. I have a natural reservation that prevents me ever really getting close to other women; sometimes I think I must have a dysfunctional gene or a neurological programming problem.

It left me feeling more alone than I should have been in a team environment, and my initial reaction was to blame myself. After all, I reasoned, it must have been my fault if somebody didn't like me. I could never put my finger on why I felt that way, but basically it's just *me*. I talk myself out of things sometimes by telling myself that I'm not good enough, that I'm unworthy. It's affected almost every aspect of my life, and created some particularly unhelpful relationship issues.

During one such insecure spell, I was at a function when I was obviously looking a bit troubled and George Pilkington asked if I was okay. I told him about my doubts, how I wasn't sure whether I was fitting in, and his reply was, "No, you can do it," and I was grateful to him for that. But a short while later I'd be sitting on my own and all my doubts would resurface, even though I knew in my heart that racing was all I wanted to do.

Why do I always have to make things so much harder for myself?

One thing that I found discouraging was the bikes we were given to race. Sandra got the latest model and Bridget and I got her old bikes; they were well put together, but Sandra obviously got the best end of the deal. I also thought that whoever did the best out of Bridget and I would get to ride the latest model at the Manx, but we were given some old nails, and Bridget actually got the better of the two. I wasn't happy.

There had already been an uncomfortable moment before this, when I refused to race at a club meeting at Darley Moor because my best friend, Jayne Sparks, had lost a pal at Darley Moor, and she really didn't want me to race there. I had met Jayne when we went to a party with a bunch of racers and friends who called themselves the 'Mallory mafia', and we'd hit it off straight away. I valued her common sense and judgement and would often give her a call when I needed sensible advice above anything else.

From the team's point of view, they wanted me to get as many races under my belt as possible because they needed me to get my national licence for the Manx. I was prepared to do everything they asked except race at Darley Moor. There were plenty of other meetings for me to get the signatures on my card, but I know they thought my attitude was a bit bizarre – after all, I wanted to go the Isle of Man, which was far more dangerous. But I didn't want to upset Jayne, so I stuck by a decision which I knew wouldn't win me any popularity contests.

So perhaps it was no surprise that I got the biggest nail of a bike. I was quite nervous when we got to the Isle of Man because I'd been there a few months earlier to support a boyfriend, Chris Moss, who'd had a horrible accident at the TT. I hadn't had a proper boyfriend at school and Chris was a biker-journalist who I had met in my first season as a racer. We started going out together but we weren't together too long before he hurt me badly.

Chris worked for *Motorcycle News* and flew to South Africa for a bike launch. While he was there, he cheated on me with one of the hotel maids, although I only learned of this when, going through his bag, I found a necklace, photographs and letters from her – they had carried on writing to each other after he had returned home. I was so hurt I ripped them up, yet when he saw what I'd done he went ballistic at me, which wasn't quite the reaction I had been expecting.

The stupid thing is I stayed with him, and what does that say about me? For a lot of girls that would have been it, they'd have been off, but not me. All I can say is I was young, I had just started racing (and Chris was quite well known in racing circles) and I was insecure.

We tried to make a go of things and went together on a tyre test to Spain, although that was awful, there was just too much tension. Chris would go to bed, while I stayed up and made friends with some nice Dutch people.

Then, at the TT, Chris had a huge crash in the Production 1000 race that resulted in head injuries and a compact fracture, where the bone was left sticking out of his leg. The whole thing was very traumatic, and made particularly worse by the fact that Chris was delirious in hospital and kept talking about the maid he'd cheated on me with. He was lying in bed asking me, "Where's her necklace? Where's her picture?" I just sat there wondering, *What am I doing here?*

There I was, on my first visit to the Isle of Man when all this was happening, and I was supposed to be returning in August for the Manx. It was a lot to take in; I was still only 22 and in my first full season as a racer. When I bumped into Pete and Sandra one evening I told them, "I'm not coming back here." It was something I said in the heat of the moment, when my nerves were shot by everything that had happened. But, on top of the Darley Moor thing, they were probably beginning to question how committed I was.

Maybe I should have spoken to Sandra about how I was feeling after Chris's accident, but I never felt close enough to her to open up. I bottled up a lot of emotion and, typically, when I did speak up the words never really came out as I meant them. Instead of a troubled young rider in need of help, they probably saw me as an upstart with ideas above her station: *Who is she to tell us when and where she will ride?* People who I've allowed to get close enough will tell you that is so *not* me. But sometimes we're judged by what we say rather than what we do, and I did have a tendency to put foot in mouth – however unintentionally.

When we got to the Manx I felt under immediate pressure. We weren't going to be dropped into it gently, we were there to make history. Bridget and I were told we were going to be the first two to start practice, but I wasn't keen on that and said to Pete I'd rather go off behind somebody. I really didn't want to go down Bray Hill first.

But it was all about the PR, and I had to do what I was told.

Bridget and I did our first practice lap together but my bike wasn't handling well. I felt that Bridget, who was spending more time with Sandra than me, had the better deal. Whenever I went to the team and asked if I could change something because it didn't feel right – for example, the suspension – they'd go, "No, that's how Sandra has it and Sandra goes fast around here."

The team was sponsored by Dunlop, so obviously we had to have their tyres; yet, historically, they didn't have all that brilliant a record at the Isle of Man, although Dunlop are again the tyres of choice at the TT for leading riders like John McGuinness.

I felt my concerns were not so much overlooked as deliberately ignored, and I'd had enough. When I was out in practice, I was weaving from Ballacrye, a jump you hit in top gear, to Quarry Bends, a fast, almost short circuit-style set of bends. People were saying to me, "Aren't you scared, Maria, when you jump Ballacrye?" and I was replying, "Actually I am – this bike is tying itself in knots."

I decided I had to put myself first. It was my first time as a racer at the Isle of Man, my first time with the team, and it should have been an exciting experience. But I wasn't happy. How can you be expected to ride well in a race as big as the Manx when you've no confidence in your bike? So I plucked up the courage to tell them.

"You know what – I can't race the bike like this. I'm really sorry, but I'm not going out." It was a genuine call. Once they thought I was going to walk, their attitude changed completely. "Take the bike and do what you want with it," I was told. I got all the things changed that I felt unhappy with, but I knew that putting my foot down had caused further resentment within the team.

The idea behind the all-female team was commercially sound, but I wasn't really suited for it and I decided to leave. I'd wanted to do a job for them because they'd put a lot of backing into me, and it's in my nature to give something back. But I didn't think it was fair to be made to ride a bike that wasn't set up for me. So I left, and was quickly back to paying my own way and riding for nobody but myself.

CHAPTER 6

THE PAIN OF RACING

Smashing up bits of my body by crashing off my road bike in 1991 certainly wasn't a pleasant experience. But it did give me an idea of what could happen to me when I went racing.

I'd already got through the pain of breaking bones after coming off the road bike and, although it hurt like hell at the time, the lesson I learned was that your mind is conditioned to forget pain once it's gone. You'll recall how bad you felt, you can tell people how much pain you were in – but it's impossible to summon up the sensation, however intense it may have been.

Don't get me wrong. I'd love to go through the rest of my racing career without a scratch, but I've had so many injuries over the years that I accept them as part of the job. If you ride motorbikes at speed, then you run the risk of crashing – so either decide to suffer the consequences or get out before it happens.

I had plenty of crashes in my first season, so thank God

my bike had plenty of spares. None of the accidents were particularly painful, but one typical instance was at Mallory Park when I low-sided the bike and ended up in the kitty litter (the gravel trap, which is a safety measure). A marshal helped me up and, while I was sitting with him on the trackside tyres, I felt blood dripping down my chin. I came off at around 100mph and must have nutted the bike's screen as I did so, cutting my chin in the process and needing a few quickly-inserted stitches before I could go out again.

That was during the morning practice and I raced that same afternoon. There was a guy who I'd got friendly with who would sometimes help me work on my bike; he beat me that afternoon, but couldn't take any credit because all his mates were teasing him that he'd only beaten the girl because she'd crashed in the morning.

In that first year, I often had more problems during practice than actually racing. People would spot the ponytail for the first time, see a girl's name on the leathers and tell themselves they *were not* going to get done by me – they didn't want to lose to a girl. I'd out-brake them, which would wind them up; they wouldn't want it happening again, so it meant everything to them to out-brake me the next time – and when that wasn't possible, they'd crash into me. I've picked myself up and screamed, "What the hell are you doing?!" in blokes' faces, wanting to hit them. On one occasion at Mallory Park, I got taken out deliberately and tried a different tack: I walked over to this guy and tried to shake his hand, telling him, "Well done, good riding! You did well to take me out there," but he wouldn't look at me. He never got to finish the race, but, more importantly to him, he had made sure that I didn't either.

My mum and dad saw one such incident after they started coming to the occasional meeting. I was at Donington and had qualified well, so I felt good going into the afternoon's race. Then, coming into Coppice, a tight corner, this guy just took me out. Some of these guys see a ponytail in front of them in the same way a bull sees a red rag. All I wanted to do was lump him, so the marshals sat us on bales on opposite sides of the track. (I know similar accidents happen to the guys, but they do happen *more* to me.)

Fortunately, I didn't suffer any physical harm. But then I went to Mallory Park in 1997 and got my first broken bone through racing; it was my collarbone and I'd never known pain like it. It hurt far more than when I'd broken those bones in my first road crash. I was riding in the Honda CB500 Cup championship and was out on track with Jimmy Miller, who worked for one of the biking magazines. He was a big guy but a bit of a hippy, and we kept dicing at the Esses, a corner which is tighter than it looks, with him getting the better of me and then me getting back at him. He couldn't shake me off and I guess he got fed up of having to overtake me, so, as we were going through the Bus Stop chicane, he hit me and knocked me off – I can't recall Jimmy ever apologising to me for that.

I landed heavily on my shoulder. I knew instantly that I'd broken my collarbone. The marshals and medical team were there quickly, helping me up, fussing over me and asking, "Are you alright, love?"

I made sure I didn't cry as they loaded me into an ambulance. When we got to the medical centre it was packed – these bikes had their limitations because they hadn't been designed as race bikes and there were a lot of crashes that day. The nurses were stressed because they didn't have anywhere to put the only girl racer, and were running for sheets to hang up and give me some privacy. I was like, "Don't worry about that – just get me some painkillers!"

They wanted to cut my leathers, but I wasn't having that – I'd paid too much for them. I told them to give me a few tablets, or an injection, and we'd take them off the normal way. When you break your collarbone you feel as if you don't want to let go of your arm because the weight resonates back through the broken bone, and I knew taking my leathers off was going to hurt. But they meant more than some temporary pain, so I bit my lip and slid out of them, managing not to cry.

(I've still got those leathers. I've also broken my collarbones on either side twice since.)

Tina came in the ambulance with me, while Dad went off to get the car and drive to the hospital. He was so upset by the accident and everything that was going on around me that he began feelings pains in his chest – the stress had brought on an angina attack. So I had Dad to worry about as well as myself, and when I was recovering it struck me that this was a very good reason why I shouldn't encourage my parents to come and watch.

Dad was checked out and, thankfully, was okay to return home, taking me with him. But it was awful. I couldn't wash myself properly, style my hair or deal with any of the everyday things you normally do without a second thought. I was grumpy. I was so nasty to my mum, when all she was doing was trying to help me. But I hated the way I had to rely on her so much to do things that I should have been doing for myself. I am not a good patient, and all I can say to her is that in such circumstances even the most trivial things can create a flashpoint and strain a relationship – it was never anything personal.

I didn't need an operation, thankfully. It took around six weeks for the bone to heal, but it was never the same again. My shoulder was shifted around and it doesn't look right, one sits in front of the other, although I hide it quite well. I did have physiotherapy through the NHS, but it wasn't enough. I decided that next time – if there was to be a next time – I'd need better aftercare.

I couldn't wait to get back to racing though. This accident wasn't going to stop me. I think some people thought that, because I was a girl, that was going to be it – my first proper crash would break my resolve. They seemed surprised to see me back, but then they didn't know me. If anything, I returned a bit stronger and a bit more determined. I wanted to show everyone that I was tough enough not to let something like a broken collarbone stop me.

My first race back on the track was at the CB500 Cup meeting at Snetterton, part of the British Superbike Championship. But I hadn't had enough time to fully recover, physically or mentally. My shoulder was still sore, my leathers felt too tight and I was very nervous. It rained and I was rubbish, the only consolation being that at least I proved I had the mental strength to get back on a bike and race.

CHAPTER 7

CLOSE TO DEATH ON THE ISLE OF MAN

At the start of 1999, I was living in Ickleford, Hertfordshire, and working again as a veterinary nurse in Stevenage. Because I wanted to race, I needed a job that gave me the weekends off.

At Donington Park that spring, I met Darren Wilson, a biker from Barnsley who was at the circuit as a mechanic. We started a long-distance relationship in which we'd get together when racing would allow; if I wasn't racing then I'd go up to stay with him, or he'd come down. We quickly decided we needed more than that, so I applied for a job at a veterinary hospital in Sheffield and moved in with Darren, who worked as a pharmacist in a private hospital.

We moved in together, but it was too soon. I'm not very good at relationships and things quickly got a bit rocky. We began arguing and doing our own thing, going out on our own, but when I told him I wanted to ride at the TT for the first time he said he'd be there for me both as my boyfriend and mechanic. All I needed to do was get a bike and my entry accepted.

I was riding in the Honda Hornet Championship at the BSB. I said to Roger Harvey, the race boss of Honda UK who I'd got to know, "Come on Roger, I really want to race at the TT," and everything happened from there. He spoke to someone at GT Motorcycles and I was given a Fireblade to take with me to the Isle of Man. We only had a month or so to get it together, but it was manageable, especially as I had a former world endurance team, 3til3 Racing, putting the bike together for me.

I'd been to the TT before as a spectator when Chris Moss had banged himself up quite badly. I'd also ridden in the Manx Grand Prix, both with the all-girl team in 1996 and again in 1998, which was one of my better years. I'd ridden short-circuit in 1997 for a bike shop in Letchworth called Jay 'n' Are, but they went into liquidation halfway through the season and everything came to an abrupt end. For 1998 I'd got new sponsors, a bike dealership in Norwich called CJ Ball & Sons, and I was riding in the Honda CB500 Cup which was being run at British Superbike meetings. I competed in the championship, which was obviously dominated by male racers though they ran a ladies' cup, which I walked away with – although it was a bit of a joke, as there were only three of us in it. I was in the top ten of the championship at one point, but dropped down when I missed a few rounds to go off to do the Manx.

Around that time, it had become fashionable in some quarters to diss the Isle of Man. There were people saying it wasn't where you should be if you wanted to make your way in racing. But I never listened, because I reckoned – and still do – that the promoters work really hard at making it what it is. The big teams are there; it attracts hundreds of thousands of spectators; it can boost your profile and earnings and, if you're lucky, lead to better things. I certainly saw it as a chance to make more of a name for myself, to hopefully be taken a bit more seriously.

When I put myself up for something new, I like to catch as much of the buzz as I can. So, although I knew I was there to race, I didn't want to just 'get in the zone' and ignore everything that was happening around me. There were too many new experiences to be had.

There used to be a huge building on the Isle of Man shaped like an aircraft hangar – not as wide but very tall – and the Honda riders used this at their TT base. I got myself a little corner of it and I loved just wandering around, watching how other riders and mechanics worked on their bikes, trying to pick up a few tips. They all seemed very efficient and professional, and I certainly didn't feel as good as they looked because the Fireblade was a big old thing – especially in comparison to the newer models today – and it would weave and not handle too brilliantly. I remember chatting to Nick Jefferies, the uncle of the legendary David Jefferies and a former TT winner, to try to get some advice on how to set it up and get it handling better, but I never felt comfortable on it.

But I was determined to race and, on the day of my 26th birthday, I took to the start line for the last lap of practice. As always, we were to set off in twos; this time I was paired up with a South African guy called Blair Degerholm, who went on to finish seventh on his Kawasaki in the Lightweight 400

TT. I had no such luck. I got the jump on him down Bray Hill, so he decided to overtake me at the bottom of the hill where there's a slight kink, but instead of going clean past he clipped me and sent me flying. I skimmed across the track and rattled up a garden fence. I was knocked unconscious – my helmet was wrecked, even the visor had been smashed off, but it did its job and prevented my head from being caved in.

Thankfully, I don't remember any more until I woke up in hospital with a broken pelvis, broken ankle, broken collarbone and too many other cuts, bumps and bruises to count. This time there was no argument when they cut my leathers off – I wasn't even conscious.

The Isle of Man is the most amazing place to race, but if you go there you have to accept that the circuit is completely unforgiving and, unfortunately, too many racers have come off their bike, some paying the ultimate price. I guess that can add an edge to the racing, but you have to put that to the back of your mind. However, that isn't always easy to do, and I had to deal with all these people visiting me in hospital, telling me how I'd nearly died. They all had the best intentions, but it mucked my head up a bit. It played on my mind for a long time afterwards, and I'd defy anyone to not think, 'What if ...' under the circumstances.

I seemed to wake up angry in hospital, and I stayed that way. Once I was well enough to have visitors lots of people came to see me, including the clerk of the course. But the cause of the accident was just skated over. I was lying in a hospital bed, smashed up, while he was able to just carry on racing. I'm a realist, and I accept that most crashes are your fault no matter what you try to tell yourself – you can blame it on the tyres, the weather, bad luck, whatever, but you're riding the bike and you're the one in charge. If another rider does something stupid, it's up to you to react and manage the situation. But I was the injured party, and I was struggling to come to terms with my first TT being over before I'd even started to race.

That crash left me in a mess, physically and mentally. I was black and blue, the bruising was everywhere – backside, legs, back, arms. But it was only temporary and I knew it'd heal itself. What troubled me were the long-term consequences of the broken bones. Was my racing career now over?

I'd broken my pubis bone, but because it hadn't displaced they left it to heal on its own. The break in my ankle was in the talus, which can be a bit dodgy because it's a bit like the scaphoid, the tiny but crucial bone in your wrist, in that it only carries blood from one direction and the part that comes away in the break can die, which then affects mobility. And, of course, I'd broken my collarbone again. My shoulder had popped out and back in when I hit the fence, but again they decided to leave the collarbone to heal of its own accord. The combined effect of the injuries was that I had my left arm in a sling and my right leg in plaster.

They have since built a posh new hospital, but I was in the old one at Douglas which was definitely past its 'best before' date. I was in the small ladies' ward and, as I lay in bed at the start of the following week, I asked for the radio to be put on so I could listen to the race commentary, but the couple of old ladies in there with me said no. So I got wheeled into the men's ward to listen to their radio. I really wanted Iain Duffus to do well, but in a pit-stop they couldn't get his wheelnut on and it cost him the race.

There wasn't a lot the hospital could do for me, other than make me comfortable. I'm not the most patient of patients, and I couldn't wait to get off the island. I was discharged a week or so later and taken onto the ferry in a wheelchair. I was returning with Darren, who had stayed on with me, while one of the mechanics from a British Superbike team drove my van, which was pretty empty. The bike was beyond repair and I never saw it again.

Mum and Dad had had not come to the Isle of Man, and one of the first things I requested when I regained consciousness was that nobody tell them anything. Unfortunately, the hospital had already telephoned them, so then I had to convince them that things weren't as bad as they seemed. They came up from Spratton to meet me off the boat at Liverpool, but I went back to Sheffield – which was a bad mistake and the start of some big issues for me.

For a start, it was impossible to get around. I needed crutches to walk because of the plaster on my broken right ankle, but I couldn't use them because my left collarbone was broken and my arm was in a sling. Although he'd stayed on the island with me while I was in hospital, Darren wasn't any good at helping me when we got home. He'd go out to work and leave me to my own devices, then come home and go out on his motorbike. I was all but trapped in my bedroom, isolated and angry.

I couldn't look after myself properly, and even going to the loo was an ordeal which would involve me having to slide off the bed and shuffle along the walls, using my one good arm for balance as I dragged myself on one leg. I felt helpless, as low as I'd ever been in my life. Making myself something to eat was just as difficult, and besides, I'd lost my appetite. I couldn't be bothered to eat and lost over two stone in two months. There hadn't been a great deal of me to start with. I was just thankful we lived in a ground-floor flat and there were no stairs, otherwise I dread to think how I'd even have got to the bathroom. Not that I could wash my hair – I couldn't lift my arms above shoulder height.

Although I could chat with family and friends on the phone, most of my face-to-face contact with people was when I had a hospital appointment and they'd send a car for me. The people who worked in the fracture clinic became my mates. I had my cast changed a few times because it was tight and pinching, and I'd go in there to have a good cry at them. I was desperately unhappy.

I don't know what would have happened if it hadn't been for my mate Jayne Sparks. I valued her common sense and judgement, and would often give her a call when I needed sensible advice above anything else.

This was one such time. I'd just about hit rock bottom, I couldn't see how things could get any worse. One evening, when I answered the telephone to Jayne, she only got as far as saying 'hi' before I burst into tears and told her I couldn't carry on like this. I could hardly speak for crying and she said, "I'm leaving now to get you and take you to your mum's." She drove from her home in Hertfordshire to

Sheffield, threw some of my belongings in her car and drove me back to Spratton.

This was my first big accident as a racer, and I really didn't handle things very well. Mum was shocked by how much weight I'd lost and did her best to help, but I must have been a nightmare to deal with. I'd get angry for no reason and just start shouting at her. I'd try to have a shower but, because I couldn't stand, I'd sit there saying that I wanted to go back to hospital. I told her I hated her cooking, although I never felt like eating, and I was angry because I could not get out of the house. There would be times when Mum was in tears and she seemed to blame herself, yet none of it was her fault, and I've tried to apologise a million times since.

But at the time there was nothing I could do but sit at home and stress out. I felt I had plenty to worry about. I'd only started work in Sheffield a few months previously and was scared I was going to lose my job; I worried about my relationship with Darren, because we'd drifted so far apart yet were finding it hard to let go; and most of all, I worried about whether I'd be able to go racing again. My body had taken such a battering that I wasn't sure whether getting on a bike would be possible.

Although I gave my mum such a hard time, moving back home was the best thing I could have done – who knows how things would have ended up if I'd stayed in Sheffield? Despite my dark moods, Mum and Dad would sit and chat with me, do my errands, try to help lift my spirits, and when Darren offered to come down one weekend to drive me to the British Grand Prix at Donington, they encouraged me to go.

We had started drifting apart even before the accident, and obviously I was disappointed at the way I'd been left alone in the flat for long spells, despite being unable to do very little for myself. I didn't see how we could have a future together, but I was desperate to get out of the house and agreed. Darren's plan was for a nice trip away together, just the two of us, and he wanted to sit with the spectators at the circuit and not go into the paddock, where my friends would be interested in how my recovery was progressing. I guess he wanted me all to himself and, being in a wheelchair, I wasn't in much of a position to argue – even though it would have meant a lot to me to visit the paddock.

However, plenty of people saw me sitting in the chair and came over for a chat. They'd say, "Is that it now, are you giving up racing?" and I'd be like, "Of course not – I'll be back before the end of the year." Darren had brought along a picnic and got quite frustrated at what he obviously saw as intrusions into our quality time together.

The broken bones did finally begin to mend and, a few months later, I was able to return to Sheffield and to work. I walked into the vets on my first day back and someone said, "Maria, is that you?" I'd lost so much weight that my uniform was miles too big, but I'd come to love the feeling of being skinny. I was down to seven and a half stone and had only just started to regain my appetite. Although, deep down, I think I was aware I couldn't carry on losing weight at such a rate, I also got a kick out of being so thin. I'd look at myself in the mirror and tell myself how well I was looking. I'm a female and I guess it's what we do, as I've got a crappy self-image and

I've always fretted over my weight. Before the accident I'd gone up to a size 12 and that made me feel podgy, so at size eight I felt much better than I must have looked.

I moved back in with Darren but things weren't good between us, so we finally agreed to split. But I had my job in Sheffield, a city I love, so I decided to lodge with a woman who was renting out a room in her house.

I got a bit more focus back into my life after I started seeing a counsellor, something I should have done much earlier. I was determined to get fit again and get back on a bike, although once again I didn't have enough physiotherapy to help the recovery. In recent years I've built up a great team of people around me – including a physio, conditioning coach and hypnotherapist – and these people make a big difference to every aspect of my life. I deal with injuries much better now, but after the TT I spent so long moping about that it was much harder to get everything going again. My therapy was little more than getting back in the gym to do my own thing, or going for a walk, and when I did eventually get back on a motorbike I felt very stiff.

Once I started coming out of the deep hole I'd dug for myself, I set a target of riding before the end of the year. Becoming more mobile helped raise my spirits, and I was determined to prove to myself – and to everybody else – that I could race again.

I wasn't able to cut myself completely free of Darren, so we saw each other on and off over that winter. But I also became friendly with a guy called Roo Piggott, who owned a little recording studio and was a keen biker. He'd got in touch after reading an article about me in a Sheffield paper and said he'd like to help, so I'd go along to his studio and listen to him make music. He became a shoulder to cry on.

By the end of the year, there was no doubt in my mind that I was going to be racing again. I was still feeling the injuries, but I persuaded Cusworths Bikes in Doncaster to give me a Fireblade and decided to race in the 2000 British Superstock Championship against all the top boys: David Jefferies, Matt Llewellyn, Glenn Richards, riders with proper teams and massive budgets.

I kept telling myself that 2000 would be a much better year for me. And it was shaping up that way, until I went and busted myself up big time at Silverstone.

CHAPTER 8

A SILVERSTONE SMASH-UP!

The counselling helped me deal with all the anger I still felt over the TT crash, and also forced me to take a serious look at my weight loss. As much as I might have enjoyed the feeling of being so thin, after talking it through I came to see that it wasn't healthy to have lost as much weight as I had. So I put a couple of pounds on in the early part of 2000, but there was no way I was going back up to anywhere near ten stone again. I wasn't feeling *that* good about myself.

Roo proved to be a real rock, while I also kept in regular touch with Jayne Sparks. That helped. We've got the sort of friendship in which we might go months without speaking, but when needed we're there for each other. As I prepared for my return to racing I'd often be on the phone to her, in tears – she'd tell me to stop bawling, stick some makeup on, get out on the bike and show everybody what I was made of. That was just what I needed to hear.

I work hard to motivate myself, but we all need to hear a few positives occasionally. Especially me, as I'm too much of a thinker – I'll sit down and think myself into believing, *I'm rubbish, look at all the times I've cocked things up*. In my world, you have to act tough, yet I'm not anywhere near as tough as I make out, and that pretence does take its toll. There are times when the last thing you want to do is put on a face and deal with all the crap, but you just have to get on with it.

Looking ahead to the British Superstock Championship, one of the teams said they'd prep my bike for me and take it to meetings. All I'd need to do was sort out a mechanic. My financial position meant I was never going to keep up with the top boys – I was probably the only one on the grid with a true stock bike, and I didn't have all the advantages that being part of a team entailed. But it still felt good to know I'd soon be back racing, in a good series.

My first race saw me finish well down the field, and I had to accept that my return to racing had been rushed. I could have done with more recovery time after such a serious injury but I'd been desperate to be in that first race, despite my ankle still clicking and a lack of conditioning in the gym. I'd got back on too quickly for my own good, but I guess I was trying to prove a big point.

I'd also had enough of people telling me that the crash was a warning, that it was time to stop racing and give up the dream. These people only wanted what they saw as the best for me, but I saw it as another bout of negativity. It made me even more determined to prove them wrong.

And of course racing was still my escape: I put my leathers on and became a different Maria, a woman who felt there was real purpose to her life. I forgot all the things that can go wrong and switched off, all I needed to do was push my bike as fast as it could go.

Unfortunately, my job at the veterinary practice wasn't going too well, which was pretty much my fault. I wasn't dedicated enough; I was only working to get through to the weekend. They hadn't had the best of experiences with me either, paying all that sick pay while I was off for months. I'm sure they were hoping for the same as my mum and plenty of other people, that the crash had taught me a lesson and I was going to give up racing. When I said I was going to start riding again, nobody really said anything; but when I announced I was leaving, I'm sure they were pleased to see the back of me.

My landlady worked with a company that made veterinary instruments and got me a job there. It started well. The working hours were much better in terms of freeing up time for my racing. I worked flexible hours that meant I could go in as early as I wanted, work through lunch and finish by early afternoon, giving me plenty of time to do my own thing.

Unfortunately, my landlady turned against me, which was a big problem as I both lived and worked with her. I never did anything to wind her up, so all I can assume is that she was jealous – as my life picked up, she may have resented a woman who, as she saw it, was pushing the gender boundaries and getting what she wanted. I started seeing a guy called Rob Frost, who was a racer and a journalist for *Fast Bikes*. It was nothing serious, but I started getting invited on some of the road tests, so I'd ring work and ask for, say, the next two days off. My boss was fine so long as I made up the hours, but this woman and a few others must have decided I was enjoying life a bit too much for their liking. They became increasingly unpleasant towards me, complaining about both my time off and my work itself. It was obvious they wanted to push me out. They were horrible, a coven of witches, so I took note of what they were trying to do and left.

Of course, I still had the problem of renting a room from one of them, and having left my job in such circumstances I told myself I'd better speed up my plans to find somewhere else to live. With Rob's help I started doing a few bits of writing and testing for magazines, while continuing to race Superstock. I loved it. Rob was known as a crasher in the racing world, but he'd set up my bike for me and I was going faster and faster with each race.

I was well down in the championship standings, but I'd expected that. I had accepted the fact that I didn't have the resources and backing to challenge the top guys and I was going to be a small fish in a big pond, but I was enjoying the experience of racing against the leading riders and, just as importantly, learning some great race craft and really developing as a racer. For somebody like me, who spends most of her life doubting herself, it was a big achievement in itself.

It was also good fun, one of the happiest times of my racing life. I'd taken on a girl mechanic called Treacle, who was not only very good at what she did but also a big laugh. It was great for me to be working with another female who shared my interest in racing, and she became a good mate. She had a boyfriend in the paddock, knew her stuff and was well into it, and it was so unfortunate that our little team would be brought to an abrupt end by another big crash at Silverstone that July.

My deal with Cusworths Bikes was that I would ride the bike in the championship and give it back to them in saleable condition at the end of the season. Instead, it went back in several boxes after being ripped up in a crash. It couldn't have come at a worse time, both for my mental health and my career. I'd been improving race by race and qualified 23rd a short while previously at Oulton Park, which was amazing. It then started raining and I crashed, a little low-sider that didn't matter, but I still got a lot from it as I'd qualified ahead of some of the top blokes. On the grid before the start of the race, one of them got off his bike to say, "You did pretty well in qualifying." "I know," I said. Maybe he'd come over just to have a friendly chat, but I felt he was trying to psych me out. Would he have got off his bike for one of the guys?

Oulton Park is a demanding circuit and, because I was riding a big bike which was physically demanding, I ended up with pump-up – a build-up of fluid in the muscle around my wrist, which made it extremely difficult to move my hand from the throttle to the brake and back again. It was uncomfortable, but I just put up with it because I was going faster each time I got on the bike. Coming from the little CB500s and Hornets, it was brilliant to be learning on a bike which could go so fast. I was a long way from the front, but I wasn't out of my depth.

I turned up at Silverstone in a nice little Volkswagen campervan that had been fitted with a transit engine. It was great to drive and was also to be my accommodation that weekend. Treacle was also staying at the circuit, and on the Friday evening I told her about a married racer who had been coming on to me. "What if I tell him to meet me and we hide around a corner to see if he turns up?" He did. So I called him and said I couldn't meet him there and that he should go somewhere else, which he did. We had this guy wandering around the paddock looking for me, and we were giggling like a couple of schoolgirls.

He actually rang me back the next day, although by then I was in hospital waiting for an operation. "That serves you right for sending me on a wild-goose chase!" he told me. He's since got divorced, something that should have happened far sooner than it did. (He'd said that I should give up racing too, as I was always hurting myself. I have to admit there were odd moments, following that crash, when I began to think he had a point.)

The accident happened during qualifying. The course has since changed, but there used to be a tight corner at Woodcote, which was the last one before the start-finish straight. It was really quite fast, although they've put in a chicane to slow it down.

I'd gone out just as it started raining and, as I came out of the corner, I high-sided the bike, which sends the rear tyre spinning up, the bike loses its grip and the back end slides away from you. Then the wheel touches down and grips again, so the energy produced by that movement forces you out of the seat and I got chucked off. The rumble strips at Silverstone are really vicious – they're designed for cars, not bikes – and I landed on them, which only made my injuries worse.

The bike stayed upright and carried on to hit a concrete wall. It got so smashed up that people who saw it being recovered were convinced I must be dead. There was coolant in the water system that spilled onto the track, causing a load of hassle as it isn't allowed and should have been taken out. Later on, I nearly got fined for that – although at the time it was the least of my worries. I was on my back at the side of the track, waiting to be scooped up and put in an ambulance.

My right wrist was a horrible mess and my right foot was in agony. I was taken to the medical centre, where a doctor took a quick look at my injuries and said I needed to go to hospital. By this time, Treacle and Jayne had arrived at the centre to hear the doctor say he was sending me to Northampton General. I told the girls I definitely didn't want to go to Northampton, as I felt they hadn't properly cared for my dad after his heart attack. I moaned at them all the way in the ambulance, but I was right.

Initially they refused to x-ray me because I hadn't had a period for several months. I tried explaining this was because I'd lost so much weight the previous year, and that I definitely wasn't pregnant. At first they weren't convinced, but I counted back to my last period and told them I'd be just about ready to give birth! Eventually, they did x-ray me, although, just as I was being wheeled in, Jayne fainted and had to be taken outside for some fresh air. She wasn't aware at the time, but she was the one who was pregnant.

The x-rays came back and somebody said that I'd really wrecked my wrist. *Tell me something I don't know*, I thought. "So what are you going to do about it?" I asked.

I was told that I obviously needed an operation, but when I asked for a bit more information they got snotty.

"Do you want to speak to the surgeon?"

"That's a good idea," I snapped back.

An A&E doctor tried to shut me up by saying a broken wrist wasn't all that unusual. But I told him to get the surgeon, who came in to tell me he wasn't very happy at being called out to speak to a patient. English obviously wasn't his first language and we both had trouble making ourselves understood, which was a concern for me as I wanted to be able to communicate with the guy who was going to put my wrist back together. If it went wrong, I knew I wouldn't be racing again.

He said he was going to put rush pins in my wrist and I bolted upright, causing Jayne and Treacle to take a step back. "We don't even use those in animals these days! I'm not having rush pins in my wrist, I want to be able to ride a motorbike again!"

"I don't think you'll be riding again anyway," he said. I told him I wanted a second opinion and off he went.

One of the people working there overheard all this and, after the surgeon left, came over and said he had worked at Oxford with the trauma team. If I wanted to go there, he'd make a few calls. Those in charge at Northampton didn't like that and faffed about, saying they couldn't get an ambulance for six hours. So Jane took me in her little Triumph car, driving back past the Silverstone circuit as we headed down the A43 while I tried to keep my arm stable. We didn't get there until gone ten in the evening, but they were fantastic, their attitude was a complete contrast to what I'd been exposed to a few hours previously. They took a load of x-rays and said they were going to get a top guy to work on my wrist.

The specialist came and spoke to me, and then the anaesthetist asked if I wanted a nerve block in my arm. I said no, because there is always the risk that it can kill the nerve, so an anaesthetic would do. The operation started at around midnight and went on for a couple of hours.

They put a Herbert screw in my scaphoid and eased my carpal tunnel, because they were concerned that the dislocation could cause a blockage that might mean big trouble. They did an excellent job, the sort of repair work that top racers have done by specialist surgeons, but if I'd have settled for rush pins I'd probably have had to quit racing.

They also operated to repair the fourth finger of my right hand, which had snapped when I landed. I'd broken a metatarsal bone in my right foot too, but they decided this would heal without surgery. Unfortunately, it didn't repair itself in the way it should have, so a year later I had to return for a bone graft that needed to be screwed in.

It was while I was in my hospital bed, coming round from the various operations, that I was told of the death of Joey Dunlop. Joey was a legend, known as 'King of the Road', winning a record 26 TT races as well as the Ulster Grand Prix 24 times and the TT Formula One world title on five consecutive occasions. Having already won the 750cc and 600cc races at a meeting in Tallinn, Estonia, he died in the 125cc race when his bike left the wet track and hit a tree. He was 48 years old.

I'd only just been told about it when my mum turned up at the hospital. As soon as she saw me smashed up in yet another hospital bed, crying, she started bawling herself. I was really harsh to her, telling her to stop crying or go home. I didn't want a big thing being made of my injuries, and I certainly didn't want anyone crying over me – especially after the sad news I'd just been given.

When I'd broken my ankle at the TT, they had put a cast on my lower leg that I'd absolutely hated. I couldn't wash, it itched and when it came off my leg was left looking like a little stick. (My legs are skinny anyway, but the muscle deteriorated horribly and it took me a long time to get it back into shape.) This time I asked if I could have a removable cast, just so I could wash my hand; they agreed, although I was told to be very careful. "If you don't spend the next six weeks completely resting it and letting it heal, you might not be racing a bike again," I was told. "I will," I replied, "but don't worry, I'll look after the wrist."

This is a fairly common injury among bikers, and I chatted to some other racers to check how their recovery had gone. One guy who'd experienced something very similar said he'd never regained full movement of his wrist, but it didn't matter because he could still race a bike – all he did was use his elbow a bit more than before.

I wanted to get as much movement as I could back in my own wrist, not only to race but because I'm right-handed. I did everything I could from as early as I could – physiotherapy, osteopathy and occupational therapy – going at it for months after the plaster came off. The girl who oversaw the treatment was really switched onto the fact that I was a biker who wanted to ride again, and she found all these extra exercises to develop my grip and wrist strength. When I came out of the cast I had no movement in my wrist, but through working with her I got it pretty much back to how it was before the accident.

I'd missed so much time over the previous couple of years through injury that, although I appreciated the need for patience, I was still desperate to get back on a bike. My recovery went so well this time that I gave myself a chance of making the TT – although, with the first one completely trashed, I didn't think I should ask for another bike from Cusworths.

I also moved in with a group of lads. I'd met one of them while I was working at the veterinary instrumentation company, which overlooked a Safeways car park. This lad was always in there practising on his BMX; he was a fantastic flatlander, and I used to watch him whenever I could out of the window. One day, during my lunch break, I walked out to the car park and sat on a low wall, watching him. We got talking. I told him what he did was amazing, and he said it was excellent that I drove big motorbikes. He was Scottish, with the great name of Magnus Sutherland Kessock, and we became pals. Pretty soon we were sharing a house as well.

CHAPTER 9

TAKEN FOR A RIDE IN THE NASTIEST POSSIBLE WAY!

After being discharged from hospital following the Silverstone crash, I was pretty helpless with both my wrist and foot in plaster. Being right-handed, I found it even harder to do everyday things for myself, so I moved back in with my parents to let dear old Mum run around after me. I was bitterly upset that a season which had started so full of promise had been disrupted by another lot of broken bones. I did begin to wonder about my luck, and tried hard to bite my tongue with Mum – not always successfully, but perhaps the temper tantrums weren't quite as personal and confrontational this time. Still, when all you want to do is race, it can be the hardest thing in the world being sat in a house with nothing to do. I'd watch TV or read, but nothing could hold my attention for long.

Although things were better in Spratton this time, I loved Sheffield and wanted to get back there as quickly as possible. I'd moved into a terraced house in Hunter's Bar with Magnus and two of his pals, but it was an absolute dive. The place was falling to bits, the central heating and water boiler were out of order more often than not, the windows were covered in mildew and couldn't shut properly, and the decor was disgusting. But there was always plenty of laughter.

I was still hobbling around when I headed back, and the lads made a real fuss of me. They said that they'd look after me, I wouldn't need to do anything, I just had to call and they'd be there for me. It sounded promising but it only lasted for a few days and then I was back to nagging them to get the Hoover out, do the washing-up piled high in the sink, clean the bathroom or tidy up the mess all over the front room.

It was cool living with these guys because there was a lot of laughter and I loved the laid-back atmosphere in the house, especially after suffering tension in my previous digs. However, these guys never watched television and I don't even know if it was tuned in because it was permanently on PlayStation, with them typically playing a fight game. But I'm more into reality stuff and I would regularly go to the ice rink in Sheffield with Donna, a nurse from the vets who I'd got friendly with. It was a good giggle, and another way of helping me regain my fitness.

Having been driven out of the veterinary instrumentation suppliers, I was having to look at what to do next. If I was going to get back on a race bike I needed to start earning money again, and then there was the small matter of paying the rent.

My injuries had healed sufficiently so that, by the end of the summer, I was able to ride a 250cc at Donington Park for a Kent-based team called DBK, but I crashed it. It was raining and I probably wasn't as strong as I should have been; I flipped off the bike and landed on my head, but I didn't break anything, so that was progress of a kind. The bike was just scuffed a bit.

I'd been a bit concerned at having to go out in the rain and asked one of the guys to give me some tips. He said, "If the bike wants to let go it will – you won't get any warning." I'm like, "Oh thanks, is that all you can say?" Yet that's exactly what happened: I was building up speed, then the back end let go and it just spat me off. I ended up with minor concussion, but woke up the next morning in a hurry to go racing. So I got everything ready and went out for a warm-up.

I'd hang out a bit with the Irish racers; I've definitely got a connection with the Irish, as my name might suggest. One of the guys racing a 250cc was named Stephen Thompson, one of those cheeky Irish types who'd do everything with a smile on his face and get away with things that other guys can't. We were going down Craner Curves when he came past me and grabbed my bum. He'd warned me beforehand that he was going to do it, but I thought he was just kidding around; I'd gone out slowly onto the track and he must have grabbed me as he went by. I had to come in because I was laughing so much. I also had a huge headache from my mishap the day before, so that was my weekend over. Despite that, DBK said they wanted me in their team for the following year on a Fireblade, so I'd be doing Superstock again.

It sounded promising. I vowed to get myself as fit as possible and got in touch with the human performance centre at Renault F1 in Oxfordshire. The guy running it at the time,

Bernie Shrewsbury, invited me along and said I'd be welcome to use their facility, which was a pretty incredible place. It was a Swedish-looking wooden building that was purpose-built and had just about every bit of equipment you could ever need. Jenson Button was with Renault at the time and I'd see him in there working out occasionally, while Mark Webber was a test driver and I'd go out cycling with him. Colin MacRae, the rally driver, was also a regular, and there were quite a few other leading sportsmen in there.

Bernie had been in the Special Boat Service and had such a big presence that he'd motivate me just by walking through the door. He used to scare me silly, but he was a great bloke and definitely helped change my approach towards physical fitness.

I was very conscious that I'd put a bit of weight on as a result of my inactivity since the crash, and not only wanted to get fitter but also thinner. I'd always used a gym, but I could be a bit lazy and didn't do as much as I should, but going to the Renault gym got me focused in a way I'd never been before. On the same day that I started using this amazing facility, I also popped into Fitness First in Northampton, where I'd been a long-time member. I bumped into David Sutton, who was a personal trainer at the gym, we got talking and he's been my fitness coach ever since.

My major motivation was getting fit for the TT. The previous year's crash and all its after-effects had done a lot of damage to me as a person. I wanted to get back there and prove to myself, as much as anybody else, that I was up to the task of racing flat out. But I was still seeing Darren on and off, and he told me that, after all the trouble of the previous year, he didn't want me to return to racing. I'd obviously been banged up pretty badly, which can't have been a great experience for him to watch, and I still had feelings for him, so I let him talk me out of it. It should have been my decision alone, but I'd decided I'd do what he wanted and not race at the TT that year.

The tie-up with DBK had initially appeared a promising opportunity, but it turned into another bad time. I was living in Sheffield and travelling down to Kent for testing and to meet with the team, but it soon became obvious that all was not as it should be. I really didn't get on with the guy who ran it, while one of his sons was a mechanic and another a rider; they had all these big ideas, the team was going to be big, there would be lots of financial backing, and at first I had no reason to doubt them. Especially when we went off testing to Cartagena in Spain and Steve Hislop was there, which was just the best thing ever.

I wasn't fully convinced that they knew what they were doing and some of it seemed to be made up as they went along, but I gave them the benefit of the doubt. At least until the first meeting of the season, when I failed to qualify and it became bad to be around them. I'm not sure what they expected but they immediately started piling the pressure on, making me feel as if I'd let them down personally, being generally quite nasty and dismissive. From that weekend onwards they seemed determined to make it difficult for me.

They stopped helping me with the bikes, they treated me like an outcast, and then the team boss sent me letters saying that if I didn't qualify then I wouldn't ride for the team anymore, but I'd still owe him a lot of money that he said he'd invested in my training.

By the time we got to Silverstone early in the summer, I was told that if I didn't qualify for that race I'd be booted off the team, which only intensified the pressure on me. When you're racing you have to be in the right frame of mind to make all the split-second decisions. If you're not feeling 100 per cent right then you're not able to give 100 per cent.

The bullying had knocked my confidence and, naturally enough, I started asking myself what I'd done to warrant it. I could certainly have done without it when I arrived at Silverstone in the summer, because you don't want to go to the grid with your mind full of doubt. Perhaps that nasty man felt it was his way of motivating me – but if he did, he'd horribly misread me. How he expected me to do my best when his team did nothing to prep my bike was beyond me. I might as well have been going it alone.

I was staying in this little caravan and, after he'd issued his ultimatum, I phoned Jayne to tell her, "I can't do this, they're not helping me, I'm not getting the support I need." I was crying, more in anger than anything else. "You know everybody in that paddock," she said, "go and find some people to help set up your bike." As always, Jayne made a complicated situation seem so simple. So I went out and rounded up four people to help me – Rob Frost, Andy Notman, Ian Cobby and Ian's partner, Jane.

Cobby was great for my head, sitting me down and helping to get me focused on what I was there to do. Jayne said she'd do my pit board, a vital link with the team that gives you all the information you need when out on the track, and any running around I needed. Rob and Andy sorted out the suspension and prepared the bike.

There was a real buzz around my bike for the first time in ages. As I went out for qualifying, the DBK bunch stood there watching as if to say, "Flipping heck, what's going on here?" I had a smile on my face again, and it was nothing to do with them. I could have used their negativity as motivation – "I'm going to show them" – but I wanted to do well for myself. I *knew* I wasn't a bad rider, and I shouldn't have been put under such pressure in the first place. A good team backs its riders, works with them and gives them the support they need to do the job properly. This lot seemed to think things were going to happen just because they were shouting and being nasty.

When I went out I was doing well; my lap times were coming further and further down, but there was a huge incident involving six bikes and so we were red-flagged and had to return to the pit-lane. Cobby continued talking to me in the pit-lane, keeping me positive, telling me I was riding well and to just keep doing what I was doing. Unfortunately, as I waited to go out again, a big, black cloud came over and, just as we went back out on the track, it started chucking it down. It was the last qualifying session and my last chance to qualify, but the rain made that impossible and I missed out by a tenth of a second.

Cobby and Jane took me into the circuit cafe for some lunch and to try to lift my spirits. We were joined by a mutual friend of ours, Gus Scott, a racer and a hilariously funny guy who is sadly no longer with us. He said to me, "Sod that DBK team – you'll find another one and they'll be much better for you." They were being very supportive, really lovely to me, but I always feel it's the end of the world when I lose a ride. I was disappointed, even though it meant I'd be free of that horrible man.

Nobody from DBK wanted to speak to me after I'd failed to qualify, so I took my stuff out of the awning and went home. I thought that would be the end of it, but a few weeks later I got a letter from the team manager's solicitors, threatening legal action unless I repaid all the money he'd paid out. We were talking serious money – thousands and thousands of pounds – and I was pretty scared; he had a team of lawyers lined up to fight me while all I had to hit back with was a bit of legal aid, and that had been pretty hard to get. I was in danger of being squashed until this guy I'd known for some time, Stan Williams, heard about what was going on and said he'd get his solicitors onto the case. Stan has been involved in the sport for many years and sponsored a number of riders; he came to my rescue like a knight on a white horse. Shortly after he got involved, the case against me was thrown out.

And so it should have been. The manager had obviously spent more money than he wanted to, but that wasn't my fault. I did all I could to help, I got all my sponsors involved and they kitted his team out. I think they were called DBK because those were his initials, but it should have been DHM: Dennis – Horrible Man.

I was delighted to get away from that team, and I was also relieved to get out of the house in Sheffield. I'd enjoyed living with the lads, they kept my spirits up and gave me plenty of laughter, but the property was beyond repair and all hope, and the landlords were not the slightest bit interested in our problems. It was time to move on.

CHAPTER 10

OVERCOMING THE REJECTION

You don't meet many outright bad people in the world of motorcycle racing. Most people in the sport – the racers, the mechanics, the teams, the sponsors – got involved because they love their bikes and want to ride them at speed. We share a common interest and – when you're lucky enough to be involved with a good team, a mechanic you can rely on and others who give you the necessary financial, emotional and practical support – you see a side of human nature that makes you feel special.

Unfortunately, there are nowhere near enough teams for the number of people who want to go racing, so there are plenty of 'privateers' around – racers who run their own team as best they can. These people make up a big part of the paddock and tend to stick together, providing help and assistance that is always gratefully received, and I've been lucky to have been a part of that.

I'd felt so guilty over what happened to Cusworths Bikes' Fireblade at Silverstone, yet Chris Hall, who owned the company, told me to forget all about it. A short while later, I got a job with Cusworths helping with their PR and Chris said to me that it was going to be a purely business relationship – they weren't going to be sponsoring me to ride. I just needed to be earning money so I was fine with that, but when I started looking around for something to ride at the 2002 TT he offered me a Honda CBR600 Sport. I think he had a soft spot for me and was just pleased to help – Chris is a genuinely top guy; his family were involved with Cusworths Bikes for more than 40 years, and I was gutted for them when the company went out of business as a result of the recession.

Tina also came up trumps by helping me get a brand new Honda Fireblade 2000 to put in the van. A new bike dealership, Avonvale, had opened up in Northampton and we went along together to take a look. I don't know how we ended up going to a bike shop together because that's something I never thought would have happened, but I'm so glad we did because we started chatting to the manager, and Tina said to him, "Do you know who my sister is? She races motorbikes and you ought to sponsor her." The guy replied, "I *do* know who she is, and we *ought* to do something." And from that I landed a Fireblade. Well done, Tina – you really did it for me that day!

Unfortunately, it didn't look like I was going to race either bike at the TT because my application to take part was rejected – the event had been oversubscribed. I had busted myself up at the Isle of Man in 1999; the following year I'd let myself be talked out of returning as I recovered from injury and then, in 2001, I'd had no chance to prove myself because the event was scrapped during the foot and mouth crisis that swept the country.

One day, while working at Cusworths Bikes, Chris Hall could tell I was gutted that my entry had not been accepted, and he said to me, "Look, Maria, you can go where water can't – if you can't get yourself sorted out for a TT entry I'll be shocked." He told me to forget about work and to, "just get on the phone and sort it out." I rang up a couple of guys who were on the TT riders' forum, Nick Jefferies and Phil McCallen, and pleaded with them to pull a few strings. Then, with really good timing, Anglia TV contacted me to say they wanted to do a documentary on me which involved filming me at the Isle of Man. I got back in touch with the organisers and the promise of TV coverage helped tip the balance.

I felt I did more than enough to warrant my inclusion, finishing 39th on the Honda CBR600 and 49th on the Honda CBR900. Those performances did my confidence the world of good, and I even felt a bit more accepted in the paddock. It was nothing too obvious, just a feeling that I wasn't being dismissed quite so condescendingly. Some of the guys started acknowledging my perpetual smile with a grin of their own; a couple would stop and chat; not quite as many turned their back on me when I walked by.

I did feel as if I'd finally arrived, and that I could also put the horror of my TT debut in 1999 behind me. As I drove home with my mechanic, Steve Whitby, we stuck all these pieces of paper on the windows of the van on which I'd written, 'I'm a TT racer.' When we were stuck in traffic, Steve wound the window down, put his head out of the car and started shouting, "She's a TT racer!"

I'd only met him five days before setting off for the TT. I went to a track day at Silverstone and Steve was there, working for one of the tyre manufacturers; we got chatting and he asked me if I was sorted for the event. My answer was, "No, I need a mechanic, can you get two weeks off?" I'd all but given up on finding anyone to help, so his offer was welcome. We didn't have a lot going for us, with not many tools and the bike still requiring plenty of work to get it ready for one of the biggest and most dangerous races in the world, while we were practically strangers who had yet to find out what made each other tick. But we had a good laugh as we travelled to the island, and established a good rapport as we worked on the bike ahead of the opening practice session.

The night before first practice, neither of us slept much. We were like a couple of kids on Christmas Eve. We had to be up really early for morning practice, which would start as early as 5am, and, as we were the first to arrive in the paddock, we sat outside the scrutineering bay. We were the only people there, so we sat down beside the bike and just laughed at each other. I said to Steve, "What are we doing here?" "Stop laughing," he said, "you're about to ride the TT course!" It was pitch black, the street lights were on, and it was quite a surreal moment.

When scrutineering finally opened up, the woman said to me, "You won't be going out on that, will you?" They weren't running a Superstock class that morning, but I told her that David Jefferies had told me he was riding his Superstock.

"He's got dispensation," she replied, as she looked over my shoulder at the rider waiting behind me. DJ was such a legend he could do pretty much as he wanted, and she made it clear I wasn't in a position to argue.

We hadn't got up at three in the morning just to turn tail and trot back to the van. So I went to see the clerk of the course, who, after plenty of begging and pleading, agreed I could take part. However, by the time I'd scraped through, the other bikes were going onto the road as practice was about to start. We quickly pushed our way through, puffing and panting. I jumped on the bike as Steve shouted for me to go out and enjoy myself. I did.

By the time I went back to the Isle of Man a few months later, for the Manx Grand Prix, I'd really started to believe that I could get my name into *Guinness World Records* as the fastest woman on the island.

The Anglia documentary had given me a boost, offering my family an insight into what I love doing and why, while I got to see how genuinely concerned they were for me every time I left for a race. It also helped raise my profile a little more, something I appreciated as I continued to chase the sponsors I needed to take my racing as far as it could go. Just because you're on TV it doesn't mean your phone is going to start ringing off the hook, with people wanting to throw money at you. But it does give you a slight edge when you need to approach people who have already been targeted by lots of other sportsmen and sportswomen, looking for backing.

And I did more than enough to justify my inclusion in the event. For a start, I took another step towards satisfying my obsession with getting into the record books, as I became the fastest woman ever to compete in the Manx; my fastest lap of 110.25mph also made me the second fastest woman in history around the TT course. It was a great meeting for me, and I was presented with the Lesley Anne trophy, which is handed out each year for the best performance by a female racer. I also picked up silver replicas for finishing 29th in the junior race and 23rd in the senior race, so the 2002 season could not have finished much better for me. And there was still the promise of good things to come in the following year.

CHAPTER 11

THE TRAGIC DEATH OF DAVE JEFFERIES

Becoming the fastest woman on the TT course was something I'd banged on about to Dave Jefferies ever since I'd met him in 1996. Dave – known to those who knew and loved him as DJ – was a legend of the sport, and it would break my heart when he was killed in 2003.

I'd first got chatting to DJ when, attending the TT as the girlfriend of Chris Moss, I sneaked onto the newcomers' bus with him. Before racing, the organisers laid on the bus to take you around the circuit so you could familiarise yourself with all the twists and turns. Having already decided that I was going to come back one day to compete, I wanted to glean every scrap of information and insight I could, so when Chris decided to take the bus tour I said I wanted to go along too.

As luck would have it, I sat in the back-row seats next to DJ. Of course, I knew who he was: the fastest person to ever lap the course, a hero to tens of thousands of bike fans. We hit it off straight away. Dave was a serious racer, the best, but he had a wicked sense of humour that really tickled me and he spent that bus ride taking the mickey out of the guy doing the tour commentary.

We became good mates and I used to love hanging out with him at the meetings. He was a massive bloke, but he was really funny and our friendship was built on laughter. He had a great family around him who used to help look after him on race weekends, and often I'd get taken under his wing. At one meeting, he told me to meet him in his motorhome because he had some lasagne we could share and he was really looking forward to it. When I turned up, he was shouting and swearing at his mum because she'd thrown it out. "How dare you talk to your mum like that?" I asked him – although I was hardly one to talk. She told him he could make his own tea if he was going to be so rude, and walked out. So he emptied two tins of beans into a saucepan and put on four bits of toast. I said to DJ, "I don't want any of that," and he replied, "I'm not doing any for you." He sat down and ate it all himself.

DJ had an infectious sense of humour and, like many true giants of sport, was far more approachable and likeable than many of those in the leagues below him. He'd won at the TT nine times in previous years, he was the first rider to complete race laps at 125, 126 and 127 miles per hour, the first rider to complete a sub-18-minute lap, the only rider in the history of the TT to complete three consecutive triple wins ... I could go on and on and on about the great man.

Yet you'd never hear him brag or blow his own trumpet. I guess his achievements spoke for themselves. He was a genuine gentle giant, as happy mixing with the mechanics and fans as he was with the other racers. My mechanic at the time, Steve, was another huge guy, around six foot six, who didn't need to look up to anybody and didn't have too many heroes. He'd never wanted to race himself but he enjoyed the involvement, he was a keen fan and he put DJ on a pedestal. He wasn't particularly shy but, whenever DJ was around, he'd go all quiet and bashful. So I used to make a point of sending DJ off to chat to Steve, just to see him squirm.

I'd hang around with DJ at most of the meetings and always felt that he was looking out for me. While some of the other riders seemed to find it hard to accept a woman in the paddock, he never had an issue with it. His status as an Isle of Man great was beyond reproach, and he wasn't going to feel threatened by anyone – let alone a ponytailed girl who looked up to him in so many ways

Over the years, I bent his ear many times about how I wanted to be the fastest woman at the Isle of Man, just as he was the fastest man. He'd tell me that all I had to do was believe it. I'm not particularly good when it comes to self-confidence, so having a guy like DJ building me up was wonderful.

I set off for the Isle of Man in 2003 convinced that, with a decent helping of the good fortune that all riders need, I'd have a crack at taking the record off Sandra Barnett. DJ was obviously racing, but took time out to ride with me around the track and pass on a little more of his experience. He'd seen me doing laps in my van so I could get to know all the twists and turns as well as I could, and told me, "Get out of that bloody van, Maria, you've done enough laps in that. It's laps on the bike you need now, and I want four laps out of you every practice session." I said I felt it wasn't possible, but he insisted and I did my best, surprising myself at how well it went.

By the time it got to the Thursday, I was feeling really tired. All those laps had helped me tremendously although maybe staying at the home of my sponsor, Martin Bullock, wasn't such a great idea as I never felt completely comfortable.

Thursday May 29, 2003 was a glorious day with beautiful blue skies, but it was bitterly cold. I said to Martin that I didn't feel too good and was going to do just the one practice lap. Afterwards, I went back into the paddock and popped into the Hailwood Centre where they do drinks and snacks with Steve. I knew the moment I walked in that something had happened, and I caught snatches of conversation about how the practice had been red-flagged and how the medical helicopter had been sent out. This is how 'blonde' I am – it didn't register for a moment that it could be anyone I knew. I just thought to myself, *I hope whoever it is will be alright.*

While we were sitting, drinking our tea, one of Martin's mechanics came over and said he'd heard that it could be David Jefferies. That was the last thing I wanted to hear, but at this stage it was only rumour with no hard facts. I said I didn't want to hang around listening to people speculating.

We went back to the hangar building where the bikes were kept and started throwing a soft ball around to keep ourselves distracted, and then I went for a walk. I saw John McGuinness, another legend of the sport, sitting with his team in the hangar looking distraught. When I went up to him to find out what was wrong, he told me it was DJ who had crashed. John had been part of the incident but, to protect me, he spared the detail and gave only a vague outline of what had happened.

DJ's family feel as if they have never got the full story of what happened that day, but the speculation is that a bike had blown up and left a film of oil on the road. So when DJ went through the small village of Crosby flat out in top gear, he skidded and struck a pylon so hard it was knocked down.

John didn't tell me any of this, only that DJ had died instantly. I was grateful for that, because my head was all over the place and the last thing I needed was the detail. DJ was such a hugely loveable guy and such a big part of my Isle of Man experience that I couldn't begin to imagine being on the island without him. I was heartbroken.

DJ's dad, Tony, had also been a TT racer, but had been in a wheelchair for many years after breaking his back in a crash at Mallory Park, just before DJ was born. He hadn't been there on the day of the accident but flew over the following day and came into the paddock, so I was able to tell him how sorry I was. I was devastated, in fact, but I couldn't bring myself to speak to his mum, who accompanied DJ to all his races, because I knew I'd be in floods of tears and she really wouldn't need that.

There was still over a week of the meeting to go, and there was some talk about whether it would be scrapped following the tragedy. But the racing went ahead, and because of that I felt like I never got the chance to properly grieve or mourn. I'd thought about going home, but people were saying things like, "DJ would want you to carry on racing," or, "The last thing DJ would want is for the racing to stop." There was so much going through my mind that it was impossible to organise my thoughts. I'd go back to my van and just cry and cry, then someone would say, "DJ wouldn't want you to quit," and I'd think to myself, *No, he wouldn't – I'm going to go out there and do it for him.*

So I went out on my Honda CBR600RR and finished 41st in the 600 Production race, which is a race for bikes virtually unmodified from those bought in the shops. It was not a pleasant experience. There was a four-hour delay because of fog, which just gave me more time to sit around thinking about everything but the race. When it was finally run it was shortened to two laps, which only confirmed my feeling that it was all pretty meaningless.

It was a difficult time for me because I'd only just lost my Uncle Len, who'd I'd been really close to and who had been such an influence on me when I was growing up. To lose two people like that in a matter of weeks hit me harder than I would have thought possible.

A few years later I had some sessions with a leading sports psychologist, Brian Hemmings, because I hadn't been enjoying my racing. I was lacking focus and motivation and my self-doubt was pulling me down. Although we'd talk about a whole range of things, the conversation constantly returned to those terrible events of 2003. Brian helped me from a sporting perspective, but it got to the point where he told me I needed a different type of counselling because I had issues I still hadn't confronted which would plague me unless I stopped running away from them. I realised I needed help and took his advice. But even now it hurts when I think about DJ.

CHAPTER 12

FASTEST WOMAN ON THE ISLAND

In the aftermath of DJ's untimely death, I did seriously think about never going back to the Isle of Man. It didn't matter what I was doing or where I was, I'd suddenly think of him and my eyes would well up. There were so many happy memories – of DJ playing around, teasing me or winding me up with that big grin on his face – and it hurt to know I'd never laugh with him again. He had this fantastic ability to put everything into perspective with a few choice words that cut to the heart of the matter. Whenever I got to the Isle of Man I'd seek him out for a chat, because he always made me laugh and feel better about myself. I might be at a meeting, uptight, nervous and frustrated that things weren't going as I wanted, then he'd crack a joke or pull a face and suddenly my problems didn't seem quite so big.

Added to all this, I had very mixed feelings about my own experiences on the island. While it's a beautiful place and one of the best locations in the world to race motorbikes, I'd had an unhappy experience there with Chris Moss when he was badly injured; I hadn't enjoyed my visit to Manx with the all-girl team; I'd busted myself up pretty badly during the 1999 TT, and I'd obviously been upset at having to appeal for a place in 2002.

Of course there had been some highs, and becoming the fastest woman ever at the Manx in 2002 was one of them. But my relationship with the Isle of Man was one of love-hate – although, despite the various setbacks, I'd still have to say I love it much more than I hate it!

While the TT takes place quite early in the calendar, typically covering the end of May/start of June, the Manx is one of the last events of the racing year in Britain. The months between the two gave me some time to gather my thoughts. Although I was still hurting over DJ, I did take some comfort from his family saying that he had died doing what he loved best. They all lived for their motorbikes and, having talked it over with lots of bikers and friends, I began to accept that for me to walk away from the sport would mean only one loser – and that would be me.

I also felt that I had it in me to go faster, and trying to claim the woman's TT record still meant a lot to me. So by the time the Manx came around, I'd made my mind up to do what everybody said DJ would have wanted and committed my future to racing.

Although I'd ridden for Martin Bullock at the TT, when I returned for the Manx I had a new sponsor and was on a Noel Clegg Motorcycles Honda CBR600RR. It was tuned by Tony

Scott, who had an excellent reputation in the racing world. I was pleased to leave Martin behind, and I think it showed in the way I rode the bike in what was possibly the best effort of my career. I finished a fantastic eighth in the senior race and, from a standing start, blitzed a lap time of 113.52mph – over three seconds faster than the previous year and little more than a second outside the fastest time ever recorded by a woman. It was a fantastic feeling. To be up there with the top guys not only justified my decision to pour my heart and soul into racing, it also showed everyone that I had the ability to ride at the highest level. It was the ideal way to bring my racing programme to a close for 2003, and I knew that a good winter and a decent bike could make 2004 a special year for me. Before DJ had died, I'd told him many times that I wanted to be the fastest woman. Now it seemed achievable – even if, heartbreakingly, he wouldn't be here to see it.

My performance at the Manx earned me a bit of attention. I received a few offers, nothing mega, but enough to keep me racing. One offer was from Stamford Superbikes and I agreed to ride for them in British Superstock, but that didn't work out. It started okay – I went testing in Spain and then to the first British Superbike Championship test at Silverstone, where there were the normal issues over the bike and its set-up, but nothing out of the ordinary. Or at least that's how I saw it, but things didn't work out and suddenly I found myself without a ride for the season.

For a while, I thought that was my TT out of the window. But all I kept thinking about was the record and how much I wanted it. So I started looking around for something else to race. I started on at my contacts, put out some feelers and eventually got an email from a guy named Dean Martin, saying that he had bikes that needed racing but his entry had been refused, so would I like to ride them?

It was the best offer I had, so I said yes. Again, it was all a bit last-minute, and I didn't actually get on the bikes until we arrived on the island – my first experience of riding the bikes was my first lap of practice going down Bray Hill!

In the weeks leading up to the TT, I jumped on bikes whenever and wherever I could. I went to Leicester to pick some up for testing by one of the magazines I was freelancing for, and a lady from the Motor Cycle Industry Association invited me along to a media day being held at Mallory Park. She told me all the major manufacturers would be there with the latest bikes, and I was well up for a go on the new Fireblade. I told her to put my name down, and thank you very much.

I was given a little card to take round to the manufacturers to reserve bikes for a specific time. Firstly, I made sure I booked my turn on the Fireblade and then secured as many rides as I could for the remainder of the day. However, in my first session, I went out on a Kawasaki ZX10 and, for some inexplicable reason, rode like a novice. I totally forgot I was on road tyres and – coming out of Edwina, which is this horrible little chicane – I high-sided the bike.

I went flying. I must been hurled at least ten feet and broke my collarbone on impact. I lay on the track and started crying, thinking my TT dream was over for another year. I was very emotional in the ambulance on the way to hospital in Leicester, but all they said was that my arm needed to be put in a sling and I could go home. "Really, is that all?" I asked the doctor. I didn't even bother to tell my family I'd been to hospital again.

Throughout that summer I'd been working hard with David Sutton, my personal trainer, to get myself in shape for the TT. A few days after the accident, I met him at the gym but he told me that what I needed was not a personal trainer but a good physio. A friend who worked on the local paper, Ashley Potter, told me about a guy named Barry Goudriaan who'd just started working for Northamptonshire County Cricket Club, and he put in a call for me. Barry was totally up for helping me out and I started having physio with him every day. It hurt as much as anything I'd ever done, but we thought the bone was healing and so I returned to the gym to do some work with David, who'd become something of a mentor to me. I'd be in agony trying to work the shoulder and he'd say to me, "Suffer the pain now for the sake of the TT, if you want to race you've got to work for it."

By the time the TT came round, however, we all knew I wasn't as fit as I needed to be. But still, there was no way I was going to pull out and run the risk of having my entry rejected again the following year.

In a way, the injury helped me mentally because I didn't put myself under any pressure – I set off with no great expectations, which is something quite rare. I'm sensible enough that I wouldn't have raced if I didn't think I could handle the bike, but I didn't have any idea how I was going to perform. So I didn't set myself any goals other than getting round and enjoying the ride.

Potentially, the team had a Suzuki GSXR1000 and a Honda CBR600 ready for me to race, but the 1000 was still in bits and they were having trouble getting it ready to run, so I wasn't so keen to ride it. I started practice week on the 600 while deciding what to do about the 1000, then Dean Martin said that perhaps he could get me a 750 to ride instead of the 1000. It wasn't really what I wanted but I didn't like the 1000 so I agreed, thinking I was getting the latest Suzuki GSXR750 model. However, when it arrived it was a 2002 version, the old shape, so I carried on riding the 600 until, on the final day of practice, Dean persuaded me to go out on the 750 just to give it a go. "Do a lap to see what you think," he told me – I did, and I loved it. It handled superbly for a stock engine, the power delivery was fantastic and I decided to race it, so I put in some more laps to get it qualified.

In memory of DJ, a ride-out was held on the Sunday before racing was due to begin and the number of people who turned out for him was astonishing. Barry, my physio, had come with me to the Isle of Man to work on my collarbone, so I took him out on the back of a road bike I borrowed from a mechanic and we joined hundreds of people in their tribute to the great man. It touched and inspired me, and I was so glad for DJ's family that they could see how much he meant to so many people.

Unfortunately, on the Monday just before racing was due to begin, the fog – which can be a problem on the island, midway between England and Ireland in the Irish Sea – came down and there was delay after delay after delay. Eventually, four hours after the race had been due to start, it got underway. But such a lengthy hold-up makes it hard to retain your focus; all the structure of the day is gone. While we were hanging around waiting to go out again, Barry worked on my collarbone and did his best to keep me mentally alert.

You started the race in pairs then, and I had a very disappointing start – the guy I was starting with was a newcomer, but it took me too long to get past him. Fortunately, the fog came down again and the red flag went up, which meant that the race had to be postponed to the next day. That afternoon in the paddock, I chatted to John McGuinness, who told me to forget about starting steady and getting my tyres warmed up. "You've got tyre-warmers on so you don't have to worry about that," he said. "Every second counts so just go flat out from the word go."

I took his advice literally and, when we restarted the next day, I left the newcomer standing to make what I thought was a decent first lap – only to see a black flag as I came into Parliament Square on my second. It had my number on it and I couldn't believe my race was over. I pulled in to be told that my torque arm was hanging off. I sat on the bike, head in hands, asking why these things always seemed to happen to me. The spectators were looking at me and I had to give myself a good talking to: *You haven't crashed, you're not injured and you're certainly not going to start crying over a torque arm.*

One of the marshals came up to me and said, "We've got races all day and you don't really want to be sat there, do you?" One of them fixed my torque arm so I could return to the paddock via the coast road, and I was leaning my bike onto the side of the van when Dean came trotting over with a huge grin on his face. "You've done it, you've done it!" he was shouting. I asked him exactly what it was I was supposed to have done. "You're the fastest woman – you've beaten the record!" he yelled. I told him he must be mistaken, it wasn't possible because my lap hadn't been that fast, but Dean was insistent so I decided to go to the press office. If I'd broken the record I knew they'd have it there in black and white.

Nobody in the press room gave a hoot. I was asking if anybody had a print-out of my time, or had a note of Sandra Barnett's record, but nobody could bothered to talk to me. I was dismissed, so I thought I might as well go back to the paddock. But, just as I was about to leave, Tim Glover from Radio TT looked up and asked me what I wanted. I said I'd been told I'd beaten Sandra's record but couldn't get it confirmed, so he got the books out and printed out my time – and it showed that I'd not only beaten her record but smashed it by six seconds.

I started crying. For a few years, my goal had been to claim that record, but it wasn't until this moment that I accepted quite how much it meant to me. Nine years earlier I'd got onto a race bike because I'd grown to realise that was all I really wanted to do with my life, and now I was the fastest woman in the history of the famous Isle of Man TT races.

It was the proudest moment of my life, even if the guys in the press room hadn't been too bothered. I'd taught myself to be a good self-publicist, something some people gave me stick for, but the simple fact is I needed to do it in order to race – without the media exposure I wouldn't have attracted the sponsors I needed – so I made sure that everybody knew about the record because I was well aware that this might be as good as it got for me.

Those nine years had been an education in so many ways, but the biggest lesson was that in motorcycle racing you can only go so far with natural talent. I'm not saying I was the best or the most gifted, because I certainly wasn't, but there were times when I reckon I could have gone up a level or two with the right support. By that, I basically mean money – if you've got it, you can basically get anything you want.

I've made my own way in racing, but it's not like I'm going to be a world champion because I'd need hundreds of thousands of pounds to even get started down that road. Where is someone like me going to get that sort of money? I have to set specific short-term goals, never more than a year ahead, and try to get as close as I can to them. My career has been all about trying to make the right choices because I've never had the resources to buy the best bikes, to go to every race meeting, to do all the testing that I need. I have to pick and choose when to practise and when to race, trying to fit them around earning enough money to keep a roof over my head and a bed to sleep in. So I spend too much time trying to beg or borrow a decent bike to race with. It hasn't made for a strong sporting career because I've never been able to achieve any great consistency, but I've had no choice.

The things that I have achieved have come almost out of the blue. The TT record is the perfect case in point: I was supposed to be riding for a different team that year, I hadn't even sat on my bikes before I got to the Isle of Man, and I was racing with a broken collarbone that hadn't healed and would later require an operation.

I can't help thinking how different everything would have been if I'd found someone prepared to back me, but those people are few and far between. I've been fortunate to have as much support as I've had over the years, but it's never been enough for me to take that massive leap forward.

CHAPTER 13

IN THE PADDOCK

One of my sayings is, "My mum worries about me racing, but she should worry more about me being in the paddock." Although I've shown a lot of determination to make my way as a racer, I always did so with a head full of doubts. Nobody needs to criticise me because I am painfully self-critical. I analyse everything I do, my mistakes really hurt and I am my own toughest critic by a long, long way.

That insecurity has been made worse by what can be a pretty surreal environment. I've worked with many good guys who I love dearly and owe plenty to. But I've also seen a side to many men – and some women – that does have a psychological effect, influencing your own relationships and your ability to trust. You see guys cheating on their wives and girlfriends so often that you can't help but ask whether your boyfriend is doing the same to you behind your back.

Perhaps it's the way some men are programmed, or maybe it's because the world of motorcycle racing is such a bizarre environment, out of sync with the everyday world. These guys know they're always going to get away with anything they do.

Tiger Woods has had all that trouble with the media over his affairs, but it was only newsworthy because the public expect golfers to behave in a certain way and live good, clean lives. It was the same for John Terry, who had so much aggro not because he was a man cheating on his wife but because he was the England football captain. Both of their roles in their own particular sport demanded that they lived exemplary lives. The outrage was not because they had betrayed their wives, but because they were perceived as letting their sport or team down.

A lot of the public perception of motorcycle racing is bullshit. Bikers are actually very dedicated sportsmen who couldn't begin to clock up lap after lap at 120mph, on something as unstable as a motorbike, if they didn't look after mind and body. But there are some racers who feel they have to live up to an image, and some who will happily sleep around because there's so little chance of them being caught or exposed.

And, to be fair to the guys, it must be hard sometimes to say no, because the temptation is always there. Even if you're not out looking for someone, there are going to be times when you're lonely, you've had a little too much to drink and an attractive woman hits on you. You don't have to be a saint to say 'no', but I can see how there are times when the guys think to themselves, *Why not? I can get away with this.*

Bikers are generally a very close-knit group, because so much of their social life is tied up with their racing – they're

In the paddock during the 2003 Isle of Man TT – I'm not sure whose car this is!
Picture by George Glue

Looking tiny in the pit lane with Neil, a mechanic, at my first Manx Grand Prix when I was riding for the all-girl team.

Right: Me and younger sister Tina pose for a school photograph when at Spratton Primary School.

Below: At my passing-out ceremony after qualifying as a veterinary nurse (with distinction) – can you spot me? I'm on the far left.

Left: I love this picture with Mum. I don't have many of us together at race meetings, but she loves coming to the endurance rounds as they are more relaxed. My Triumph had blown up and here she was just the best at comforting me. She really is the best mum ever!

Right: At Sarah's Cottage on Padgett's Suzuki GSXR750 K2 on which I set the TT lap record in 2004.
Picture by Bill Dale

Left: Cresting the Ballacrie jump during the Manx Grand Prix in 2004 when, riding Padgett's Suzuki GSXR750 K2, I flew to eighth place in the Senior Race.
Picture by EDP Photos

Right: David Sutton is my long standing strength and conditioning coach. It's strange how he gets to put me through so much pain – without me complaining – well just the odd complaint.
Picture by Paul Bryant

Left: Working with my physio Barry Goudriaan after recovering from my big crash at Silverstone in 2006.

Above: With Kevin Schwantz, one of my racing heroes.

Below: Chatting with Carl Fogarty – the most successful world super bike racer.

Above: With my hero Mick Doohan at the 2009 Goodwood Fesitval of Speed – being a stalker rather than being stalked!

Left: With racing legend John McGuinness at a Mallory Park British superbike meeting 2004 – that was the year we were king and queen of the mountains at the Isle of Man.

Above: Riding a Cusworths Bikes Honda Fireblade, prepared by T3 Racing, at the British Superbikes at Snetterton in 2000.

Right: At Bungalow Corner during the Manx Grand Prix 2003 on a Noel Clegg Honda CBR600RR tuned by Tony Scott.

Picture by John Watterson, Isle of Man Newspapers

Right: At the Southern 100 riding a prototype CBR400RR bike developed by Ricky Leddy.

Picture by Stephen Davison/ Pacemaker

Above: On a CMS Yamaha R6 at Ballaugh Bridge during the 2009 Manx Grand Prix – this was the year I got my mojo back.

Below: With Tony Morris, great guy and sponsor, and the BMW S1000RR that he so generously bought for me and which was to be raced at the 2010 TT. We are pictured outside Wollaston BMW in Northampton.

Picture by Northampton Chronicle & Echo

Above: Working at the trade EXPO show for Bering in 2005 with my race bike and leathers on the stand.

Picture by Mick Payton

Left: With Murray Walker in the Isle of Man TT press office in 2009.

Right: With my mechanic Steve Whitby in the paddock post-race at the 2003 TT.

Left: Dave Weston working on my road-going RGV250 with my race bike in the background. We must have only just got that as it has the original owner's livery still on it. How messy was that unit? But better than nothing!

Right: With Richie Freeman at the 2009 Goodwood Revival – we wouldn't normally dress like this but period costume is a must at this great event.

Left: David Jefferies winding me up in front of the TV cameras – DJ was an absolute legend and great friend and I miss him dearly.

Above: With Mum Eileen, sister Tina and dad George after receiving my MBE at the Palace – we all made it there in the end! *Picture: PA*

I shared a joke with Prince Charles when I went to Buckingham Palace to get my MBE. He asked if he had come on a motorbike – to which I answered yes!

Picture: PA

Proudly showing off my MBE after receiving it from Prince Charles.

Picture: PA

working and living together side-by-side for three or four days of most weeks throughout the season; they attend the same functions and they go to the same venues for testing. So it's easy to hide behind the unspoken agreement that what happens in the paddock stays in the paddock.

I've travelled with this circus for many years, and I've been shocked by how brazen some of the racer-chasers can be. There are groups of girls who go to meetings with the sole intention of sleeping with one of the racers, and they'll do anything they can to achieve that aim. They'll parade as close to the pit-lanes and the paddock as they can get; they'll hang around outside the mobile homes; they'll slap on makeup and short skirts and stalk out the pubs and clubs where the bikers go after racing to unwind. And the racers expect them to do it – they have no respect for the girls, they just see them as their property to do with as they wish. Just one point of a finger and it's, "I'll have a bit of you now."

Isn't that awful? The guys do it because they can get what they want, but it's not very flattering to the girls. I think it's very sad.

I look at the wives and girlfriends and wonder what makes them stay with these men. I can't believe they haven't at least got some idea of what is going on. There will always be some wives and girlfriends at any particular meeting, but none of them are there all the time, and then, as soon as they have a child, that's it – they're at home playing happy families, while he's getting up to whatever.

I know some of them are top blokes, good family guys, but they race hard and they play even harder, and racing takes up such a big proportion of their lives. I'm sure it's been like that for as long as people have been racing motorbikes – I bet that in Barry Sheene's day there were girls who wouldn't normally find themselves at a motorsport event, hanging around the paddock. Why? A lot of these racers are ugly mugs, but they've found something they're good at and suddenly it makes them sexy.

My first TT was a real eye-opener. I was in the paddock early one morning when a couple of mechanics rushed up to one of the leading riders to tell him that his girlfriend had arrived earlier than expected, and he needed to get himself 'sorted out'. I don't know whether the girl he had been with during the night was still in his motorhome, but he didn't waste a second in rushing back to it. They had a child, he was cheating on her and all he was worried about was getting caught. I felt really sorry for the girlfriend.

Many of the bikers have opinions of women that have been distorted by the antics of the racer-chasers. I've felt that in the way they look at me and talk to me. In my first couple of years on the circuit I was hit on regularly, but I realised early on that you could easily get a bad reputation that would stay with you. If a man sleeps with 200 women then he's a lad, but if a woman does a fraction of that then we know what she gets called.

I never wanted that sort of a reputation. I'd hear what they'd say about other women, how they'd snigger that one of them had been all round the paddock, and I'd think to myself, *But so have you, you filth bag, who are you to judge?* Yet with the guys it's just accepted that this is what they do.

Just as bad is the gossip. Because everyone works and lives on top of each other, the paddock is full of it. It only needs one person to say something and suddenly it's being passed on as if it's gospel. I find that quite funny. I've walked through a paddock with one of my male friends and I know everybody has been wondering whether I'm sleeping with him; then, the next week, I'll walk through with somebody else and they'll all start wondering whether I'm sleeping with that one as well. One of my team-mates used to wind me up about this something rotten. I'm quite a huggy person, so when I see someone I haven't seen for a while I'll give them a friendly cuddle, and he'd say to me, "Have you been with him?" It'd be a wind-up, but he'd get the response he wanted. And then I'd start asking myself, *Does he* really *think that?* And even if he didn't, did anyone else think it?

I've developed a thicker skin over the years, but I'm still careful how I am around some of the men. When a young girl comes into the sport, I'm keen to pass on some of my knowledge and tell them about the other side of racing that they've yet to experience. Racing a motorbike is fantastic and it's there to be enjoyed, but I don't think it hurts to point out some of the potential pitfalls, maybe mark a few cards. Although I do think that perhaps the new wave of female racers are not as naïve as I was when I came into the sport – perhaps young girls generally are a bit more streetwise now.

I've had a great relationship over many years with many of my sponsors, who are really good guys. But I've been accused of sleeping with a sponsor to get his backing, and I know it's said about other girls as well. Somebody will tell you that he knows for a fact that a girl is having sex to win support and I'm always, "No, no, no, that's not happening," but then he'll say to me, "How do you know it's not?" And of course, you can't be 100 per cent certain.

It's an easy accusation to throw at a woman and it does get you down when you come up against it time after time. I had one particular sponsor who friends kept saying was making it obvious he wanted me. I can be a little naïve at times, but I did start to feel as if he believed he owned me and I didn't like it. It's hard to give up a sponsor because they don't exactly grow on trees, but I ended that particular partnership and he went straight out and got another female rider. And then, me being me, I started wondering whether it was all my fault. Had I led him on? Was I sending out false signals?

All too often you find you're not being your natural self. We are performers, we are there to put on a show, and there is this expectation that you have to live up to the image. I try to mask my emotions by always having a smile on my face when I'm around the paddock, so much so that one racer nicknamed me 'Smiler'. But as soon I'm back in my caravan, that's when I let my guard down and the vulnerabilities come to the fore.

Sometimes I feel like I have a hidden side to my personality that only those closest to me are allowed to see. Everybody else gets the public persona, and you do need it because you'll have complete strangers come up to you and talk about the most bizarre things.

So many people are so tactless. You get it even when you're in your pyjamas in hospital! After my first bad crash on the Isle of Man I was put in a private room but, as I lay in bed, I started receiving a lot of visitors I didn't recognise. I was recovering from the accident and there would be people like marshals and spectators coming into the room. I'd have to ask, "Sorry, do I know you?"

When you experience something like this for the first time, you wonder what's going on. I accept that there is a side to me that is public property and that you need to relate to people, but I was ill and vulnerable and I found it all quite bizarre.

The nurses were just sending anybody through who asked for me by name because they obviously thought they must know me, and vice versa. I do appreciate the fact that most of them were just taking the time to show me they cared. But it did get a bit creepy when one lad, who was obviously not all there, came into the room and just stood there without saying anything. I asked him what he was doing and he asked me to tell him all the details of the accident, how I came off my bike, the damage I'd suffered, what my feelings were. I asked him to leave but he just stood there, so I had to call a nurse who chased him out.

The next day he came back but, fortunately, my boyfriend of the time was sitting with me. After that, a male nurse would vet all my visitors – they'd only get to see me if I knew them. I was grateful for that because I'd started to feel a bit like a freak show – I know I have a public persona and that gives people some rights, but it was all a bit too much!

It took me a few years to come to terms with the way that people see you as public property because you're a racer, and I think it was harder for me than for the guys because of the sex thing. Initially, I found it uncomfortable, even embarrassing, to be gawped at as I was walking along in my leathers. Although I tried to ignore it, I'd be muttering under my breath, "What are you staring at?" There are still moments now when I see people looking at me and think to myself, *Surely they've seen girls race by now?* But we still seem to be something of a novelty.

That novelty factor also made me feel I was being patronised. If I did okay in a race, I'd get all this stuff like, "You're not bad for a girl," or, "That was a good race for a girl," and it used to rile me. I'd point out that it'd be good whether the racer was male or female, and that they shouldn't be so sexist. I also discussed it a lot with my friend Jayne Sparks, and she helped me see that people generally didn't mean it in a bad way – what I saw as patronisation could actually be somebody just trying to be friendly and supportive, so there was no need to react in the way that I did. Perhaps sometimes I have taken offence when none was intended – if that's the case, then I apologise.

CHAPTER 14

FIRST WOMAN ON THE TT PODIUM

I made history in 2005 by becoming the first female solo racer to claim a place on the podium at the Isle of Man. That was a great year for me, probably the only season in my career which went pretty close to plan, with no injuries to disrupt my racing and no problems with bikes or backers.

After claiming the record as the fastest woman to lap the TT course in the autumn of 2004, I had to return to hospital for an operation on the collarbone which hadn't mended in the way it should have. This time, I asked to be referred to a surgeon in Leeds, Toby Branfoot, who had been recommended to me by one of the racers, Jim Moodie.

Toby had become a specialist in motorcycle-related injuries, so I went up to Leeds to see him and he decided I needed a bone graft. He took bone from my hip to strengthen my collarbone and also put a plate in. The physiotherapy with Barry Goudriaan went well and I trained really hard with Dave Sutton in the gym, giving myself the chance to start the season in decent shape.

I had my own Honda 600 that I was going to race, but at the start of 2005 I had a good chat with John McGuinness, who said to me, "You're riding all these big bikes, but why don't you get on a little bike and just enjoy yourself?" I'd been told this before but, because I was always trying to prove a point, I'd say, "Little ones are for girls," and I'd carry on racing the production bikes. However, John had won at the TT on a 400 belonging to Ricky Leady, a tuner, and said I should give him a ring. What he said made a lot of sense, so I rang Ricky.

"Hello, my name's Maria Costello."

"What, *the* Maria Costello?" he replied. Which I thought was a promising start.

I asked him whether he still had the bike that John had won on at the TT. Although he didn't, he said he was sure he could help me out by getting something similar. He seemed really keen on getting me on a 400 and spoke about it to Tim Bradley, a racer whose bike he tuned. They came up with an RLR Motorsports Honda RVF400, which I quickly fell in love with. It was fabulous to ride.

Even before I got on it, Ricky said to me that it would be like riding a scooter compared to what I had been riding. It was, and it was really good fun. Don't get me wrong – it's great riding the big bikes around the Isle of Man circuit, but, because of their power and size, they obviously demand more from you both physically and mentally, whereas I could ride the 400 flat-out with a big grin on my face.

I decided to take it to the North West 200, an Irish road race that takes in a triangle covering Coleraine, Portrush and

Portstewart, to see how I'd get on. It went better than I could have hoped. It was my first visit to Northern Ireland and I loved everything about the meeting – the atmosphere produced by a crowd of around 150,000 (the largest sporting event in the province), the friendliness, the circuit and, most of all, the pleasure of riding that bike. I was the third 400 to cross the finishing line and ended up seventh overall in the joint 125cc/400cc.

I was in really high spirits by the time the Manx came round, and took a great little team with me to the Isle of Man. I had a good mechanic in Andy Grimshaw, David Sutton came to offer his support and I also took this guy I was seeing at the time, Tom Caffrey. There was a real buzz to the Costello team.

It was the first time I'd ridden a 400 around the course, but practice went brilliantly and at the end of the week I'd registered the fastest time. It was amazing! A lot of people were saying to me that I could actually win the race and I started to believe it just a little.

Blimey, a girl – me – winning the Manx!

My team was solidly behind me, which makes such a huge difference. Although I told myself not to get too carried away and that the hard work was still to come, I was instilled with a confidence that I too often lack.

As it transpired, it seems that some of the guys had been sandbagging during practice – not going as fast as they could – and when it came to the race they started off with laps of around 107mph from a standing start, which I hadn't got anywhere near. When it was my time to start, I set off ten seconds ahead of Alan Oversby – a fantastic rider, with tons of

Isle of Man experience, who'd been winning on 400s for years. Because he also raced classics, he'd compete in four races at the Manx.

He quickly caught me up and I thought to myself, *Bugger, he's already got ten seconds on me!* But I was still feeling good so I decided to do all I could to stick with him – he couldn't shake me off. We raced the whole thing together and, for me, it was like having an Alan Oversby masterclass. You take a slightly different line on these bikes compared to the bigger ones so I followed him around, staying with him and learning as much as I could.

I loved every second of that race, lapping at nearly 108mph. After crossing the finishing line, I came back up the return road to be greeted by a marshal waving me into the holding area for the podium. It was only then that I realised I'd finished in the top three and that I'd get to climb up the stairs and spray champagne around. I'd been helped by the fact that the guy who was leading the race by a long way crashed out on the last lap, but that wasn't going to stop me celebrating the best moment of my racing career.

Debbie Pitts, a friend who lived on the island that I often stayed with, came over and gave me a big hug. Everybody seemed to want to shake my hand. A TV reporter put his microphone under my nose and asked me a few questions, but I was so excited I spoke at 100mph. I'm sure didn't make any sense, it probably didn't even sound like English because I was trying to get so much out in one go.

Setting the lap record at the Isle of Man the previous year had been a great high, but it didn't compare to this. The immediate aftermath to that record ride in 2004 had been an anticlimax. There was no real way of being able to celebrate it, and it was a struggle to even get it acknowledged in the first place.

This time I got to walk up the stairs to the podium and stand there with a bottle of champagne in my hands, the fans looking up at me, feeling like I was on top of the world. I remember saying to myself, *Suck this in, don't ever forget this moment.* I was smiling so much my jaw hurt afterwards.

As I went back down the steps after the presentation, I said to myself, *It doesn't get much better than this – but how great would it be to be the winner? I'll be back!*

I rounded off 2005 in great style when I received the BBC Northamptonshire Sports Personality of the Year Award in November. I was up against some really impressive sportsmen and women, and the list of nominees included the likes of Steve Thompson MBE, the England Rugby World Cup winner and Northampton Saints hooker, snooker star Shaun Murphy, who won the Embassy World title, and another snooker player, Peter Ebdon, who had added a sixth ranking title to his name.

Others on the list included Northamptonshire cricketer Usman Afzaal, the county cricket club's Player of the Year who set a record by scoring four centuries in as many games, Sally Kettle, who rowed with her mother across the Atlantic and who was preparing to do it again as the captain of the Rowgirls women's four, and swimmer Caitlin McClatchey, a World Championship bronze medallist in the 2005 400-metre freestyle event, whose relay team finished fourth at the Athens

Olympic Games the previous year. The winner was to be decided by a public vote on the BBC website, which extended right up to the evening of the awards ceremony that took place at Franklin's Gardens, home of the Northampton Saints rugby club. Nobody had any idea who was going to win – it was an evening full of suspense!

I expected Steve Thompson to win because he had the backing of a huge club in Northampton Saints, who regularly get home crowds in excess of 10,000. But when the final voting figures were announced it was revealed that I'd won with 35 per cent of the vote, with Steve second on 28 per cent and both of us going through to the regional final a month later.

I couldn't believe it when they called my name out, while my parents and Tina, who were there with me, greeted the announcement by jumping up out of their seats! It was a special moment for me. The thought of beating so many great sportsmen and women, and so many people going out of their way to vote for me, was quite humbling. So to all my family, friends and fans who made the effort – thank you so very much!

CHAPTER 15

THE WORST CRASH OF MY LIFE

Becoming the first woman on the podium at the Isle of Man got me a lot more attention than the lap record ever did. There were plenty of pictures taken, and the experience of climbing those steps to be presented with a trophy in front of a cheering crowd gave my confidence a massive boost.

There was no longer any doubt in my mind that I belonged in this world, and I definitely noticed a change in attitude among many of the guys. Plenty of them had been suspicious of me but, because it can be so hard for them to get recognition and sponsorship, I did understand some of the reasons for their lack of enthusiasm.

But the podium changed everything. It was the moment when I finally began to feel accepted as Maria the biker.

I'd always tried to be friendly to the other bikers, even after they'd turned their back on me or dismissed me with a curt barb. I hadn't really made any enemies because, when they'd upset me, I tended to walk out of the paddock and go for a cry rather than get involved in a grandstanding confrontation. I like to think I'm pretty modest about what I do, so nobody had to get past an ego to talk to me about racing and I've always welcomed the opportunity to chat to fellow racers and share experiences. But it probably helped once they started noticing me for my achievements on a bike.

Early in 2006, I was offered the chance to test for a place in the SUD Endurance 84 team for the 24-hour Le Mans race. I agreed to have a go because I thought it would be something different, but, once again, it would end up with me back in hospital.

I was given a Suzuki GSXR1000 to ride alongside team owner Luigi Mazzitelli and top French female racer Fabienne Migout – who goes by the unflattering nickname of 'the Flying Piglet', but seems to have done rather well from it. I had hardly any time to get to know them, as I high-sided early into my test. The crash happened due to the bike running standard footpegs which would drag on the tarmac and, as I accelerated out of a bend, one of them dug in and threw me off.

I didn't need a doctor to tell me I'd broken my collarbone yet again. Fortunately, I'd paid for this excellent insurance policy at the start of the year, which meant I got taken all the way back to Spratton by ambulance. I hadn't let my parents know I was on my way – what was the point of worrying them? – so they had the shock of opening their front door to a couple of paramedics on either side of their daughter!

I'd telephoned Toby Branfoot before leaving France, and he told me to get to Leeds as quickly as I could after getting back to the UK. Replacing the plate was a straightforward operation, and the one Toby inserted has stayed with me to this day. If anybody asks about it, I can show the plate to them by hunching my shoulder forward and exposing its outline.

The right wrist I'd previously broken had been hurting me more and more over the previous few months, so I asked Toby to have a look at that while I was there. He had it X-rayed and said to me he wasn't surprised it was causing me so much pain – the Herbert screw which had been put into my scaphoid had been working its way loose and had started burrowing into a ligament. So he took it out, and I woke up in more pain from that than from anything else.

It was a pain that simply wouldn't go away. I absolutely zonked myself out on morphine, asking for more and more of it. What I didn't know at the time was I should have had my painkillers changed to ones that targeted the specific nerves, rather than the central nervous system as a whole. Basically, the morphine wasn't having any effect.

I'd wanted to return to the North West 200, where I'd had so much fun a year earlier, but the pain was too much. My wrist was so sore that I lost a lot of strength and movement and it was in no shape to race. I'd also broken a bone in the tip of a finger on my right hand and, although it didn't require an operation, it still felt uncomfortable.

Somewhat ironically, the troublesome collarbone was repaired and ready for action within a week of the operation. But there was no way I was getting back on a bike just yet because of my wrist, although I went over to Northern Ireland and had a ball working with Ulster TV. They invited me over to do a bit of on-camera work for them, and it gave me a chance to experience a top racing event as other people see it.

I hardly ever drink and I never mix alcohol and riding, but this time there was no pressure on me and I was able to visit The Anchor, a famous pub in Portstewart. It was heaving, I couldn't believe how many people were there; it reaffirmed my belief that racing is a very social sport. As a rider you often have to steer clear of the parties and the beer tents, but a lot of people have a lot of fun at a race meeting. I had a lot of fun working with Ulster TV, presenting a live link after the Thursday night practice session, as well as doing a number of PR events for the organisers who'd seemed to take a liking to me the previous year.

I returned to racing a few weeks later and was pleased to finish fifth on my Bering CBR600RR in the East Midlands Racing Association's 1300 open races. I also rode to ninth place in the fiercely-contested 600SS class, and got enough out of this to tell myself I could put my injuries behind me and still make 2006 a good year.

It looked that way when I finished seventh out of the 400s and 15th overall in the combined 125cc/400cc at the Southern 100 Road Races on the Isle of Man's Billown Circuit, a tough event for solo racers and sidecars. I was up against the likes of TT legend Robert Dunlop – who would tragically die two years later, at the age of 47, after crashing in a practice session at the North West 200. Robert, who won the North West 200 a record 15 times, was the brother of Joey Dunlop who'd died racing in Estonia in 2000. Robert had temporarily retired in 2004, but he made his return a year later and was as good as ever, before his bike appeared to seize up and he high-sided on approaching the Mathers Cross section of the course in Portrush.

This was my first time in the S100 and I also took on Chris Palmer, who had followed in Joey Dunlop's footsteps by winning the Ultra Lightweight race at the TT in successive years. So I was well pleased with my efforts on this demanding road course.

The way I'd bounced back from the early season injury had given me a lot of confidence. I looked forward to the Manx Grand Prix with the hope of taking the podium again. I set off for the island thinking that, if all went well, I might once again experience the joy of walking up those steps – and if everything went better than I dared hope, perhaps I could go one or two places ahead of the previous year.

However, rather than a podium finish, I would suffer the worst crash of my career. It would not only do severe damage to my body but would also plunge me into a black hole of depression that took me the best part of three years to dig my way out of.

Practice had started well enough for me, but then I had a shock during one of the later sessions when I set off with a good mate, Andy Jackson, a plumber from Preston who'd raced in the TT several times. We hadn't been out on the road very long when we came across a crash that looked like a bomb site – someone had suffered a very bad accident. Andy's brother Alan had gone out a few places ahead of us and, as we drew level with the crash, I could hear Andy shouting, "Oh my God, Alan! Alan!" and he immediately stopped.

One of the things that is stressed to racers at the Isle of Man is that you should never stop when something like this happens – you carry on going and leave the experts to do their job. So I continued, but I was in a bit of a daze, I kept saying to myself, *That was Alan and it looks really bad*, and I was getting a bit tearful behind my helmet. My concentration had gone and it became a case of just getting back to the paddock.

Then Andy, obviously in distress, came flying past me. I tagged onto him and followed him into the paddock, where he leaped off his bike and went looking for his mum to break the news before she started picking up on the rumours.

Alan was helicoptered to hospital in a right mess; he'd smashed his leg up badly, had internal injuries and also lost a lot of skin. I went to visit him in Nobles hospital a couple of times in the following few days and, as luck would have it, shortly ended up in a bed at the same place.

Having done so well the previous year on the 400, I was entertaining a few thoughts of actually winning in that class. I'd taken another Ricky Leady bike to the meeting, a prototype fuel-injected 400, but it died on me early on. Tim Bradley, the racer whose bike I'd previously ridden, sent over his RVF400 which was an amazing gesture – he'd even had it ready for me just in case. I was riding well when, on the last lap of practice, I crashed at the Kepple Gate section of the course.

Another rider had crashed there just moments before I arrived. There must have been some oil on the road as a result of that crash, because my front tyre lost its grip without warning. Suddenly, a bike which had done nothing wrong up to that point was out of control. I shut my eyes as I flew towards a bank at the side of the track, because I knew the collision was going to hurt. I wasn't wrong – I broke my left shoulder blade, my right femur and several ribs.

I didn't lose consciousness, which was something of a mixed blessing, but I was winded and couldn't get any air into my lungs. I'd been winded in accidents before so I was telling myself to stay calm, not to panic, that my breathing would come back, but I knew I was in serious trouble with my leg. A marshal who I knew came running over and was telling me, "It's okay, you're okay," and I shouted back, "I'm not okay – I've broken my leg!"

I was really angry, shouting and swearing when the paramedics arrived and they also tried to calm me down. I've never lived it down, every time I go back there somebody will joke with me about it – I *do* try to be on my best behaviour, but breaking your leg can bring out the worst in you!

I'd managed to wedge myself into this thick bank of heather, which meant they couldn't get their board underneath me so they had to try to work my right leg free. As I've said, it's impossible to actually recall the sensation of pain, but I remember thinking, *This is* really *hurting*. Finally, they got the leg free enough to put a blow-up splint around it and strap both my legs together, but that sent another bout of intense pain through thc right one. My right foot felt extremely uncomfortable and – as I lay on the board waiting for the helicopter to arrive – I looked down my body to see the foot resting at an odd angle. I asked the paramedics if they would move it but they said, "No, stay as you are, you're fine now."

"No," I said, "I'm not."

The helicopter eventually arrived and, as they lifted me off the ground to load me in, I began to feel the pain in my shoulder. I knew I'd damaged something there. I was feeling really queasy and, though they tried to make me as comfortable as they could, there wasn't too much they could do at that stage. I just had to go with the pain.

The helicopter ride was only a few minutes, though it seemed much longer and I was afraid I was going to be sick. On landing, I was lifted out to be transferred to an ambulance and driven through the car park to Accident & Emergency, where I was lifted out to be placed on a wheeled stretcher. Every movement sent a bolt of pain through either my leg or my shoulder or both, while I also had a problem with something in my chest area – it was no longer a simple matter of getting my breathing back under control.

I was a mess, sometimes erupting into tears, and this lovely nurse, a sister in A&E, took my hand as they wheeled me through the doors. "You'll be okay now," she said, "we'll sort you out." I said to myself, *Get ready for another load of pain because they're going to unstrap your leg and cut you out of your leathers.*

They shuffled me from the stretcher to a bed, and the nurse said to me, "Can your boyfriend come in?" I didn't have a boyfriend at the time, it was a guy who was supposed to be taking me out on a date that evening.

I'd met Dave Hopkinson at the North West earlier that summer, when I'd given myself a rare treat and gone out to a nightclub when I wasn't riding because of injury, which meant

I could have a couple of drinks. They were already beginning to have a bit of an effect when this guy pinched my bum. I turned round to him and said, "You can't afford that!"

I got chatting to Dave, who came from Lancashire, and we met again when I got to the Isle of Man for the Manx. We got on well enough for my mechanic to tell me, "You keep your mind on your racing!" But when Dave said he wanted to take me out for dinner after final practice, I said yes.

Of course, we didn't get to eat. The next time I saw Dave was when he arrived at the hospital to see the mess I was in; he walked in and just held my hand. A couple of nurses turned up and said they were going to take my leathers off, but seemed to faff about for ages without getting anywhere. It was hurting like hell and the nurses were trying to reassure both me and Dave, talking to him like he was my boyfriend.

A doctor told me he was giving me a nerve block, but when he went away again I thought to myself that if I had the choice I wouldn't be having one. Sometimes a nerve block cannot be reversed and, on a previous occasion when I'd broken my wrist, I refused one, deciding I'd take my chances with just an anaesthetic and lots of morphine.

But this time they were pulling my broken leg about and telling me they were going to have to cut my leathers off, which I knew was going to hurt. So I told them to find the doctor to give me the nerve block. He returned to give me the injection before moving my leg and asking, "Can you feel that?" And I could – the nerve block hadn't worked! So it came down to gas and air, as they cut off my Bering leathers which I'd only got three days previously to wear at the Manx!

They did their job – I guess if you can go through childbirth on just gas and air then you can get through a broken leg.

I had my operation the next morning and afterwards I was put in a private ward, which was great at first. But when I had to go for some X-rays, a couple of nurses were helping me off the bed when one dropped my leg. I screamed at her and shouted at everybody else, "Don't let that woman touch me again!" I was in a lot of pain, and if there's one time in my life when I'm going to get cross with people it's when I'm the patient and I'm not being handled competently.

They put me back in the private room, and once again strangers started turning up to gawp. I didn't have a clue who half of them were, so Dave took charge of 'admissions', only letting in people we knew. But, because I'd crashed at the end of practice week, race week was still happening so all the racers were there and I had lots of lovely visitors. Mum wanted me back home as quickly as possible, but I was quite happy to be there all week.

Although the break in my leg was fairly clean, it had occurred close to the hip joint at what is known as the neck of the femur – I was told this was because the bike might have struck me after I'd been thrown off. I had a dynamic hip screw inserted, as well as a long plate to run down my leg to support the bone, which had to be screwed through it at an angle. It was performed by a surgeon called Ian Wright, although I had everything approved by Toby Branfoot over the telephone before I'd let him start.

When Mum telephoned the hospital the morning after my operation to see how I was, they said I was alright and that "her boyfriend has been with her all night." So she called Tina, who had to tell her, "Maria hasn't *got* a boyfriend."

If you break your femur lower down you can have a pin put in and often be walking three days later, but my break was too high for that – it was where that part of the femur turns inwards at an angle, when you stand up. I was in Nobles for two weeks and, shortly before I was due to be discharged, they started to get me moving about on crutches.

If things had been bad for me, it was like tripping over compared to what poor Alan Jackson had to go through. A lot of people think that if you have a crash on the Isle of Man, you'll have some of the best doctors in the world waiting there for you, but it's not true. I'm not saying anything about my surgeon because he was fantastic, but Alan ended up sitting around for several days because they couldn't do the operation that was required and they were struggling to get him a bed back home. He had to wait longer than he should have to be treated, and his crash left him with one leg shorter than the other and a limp (although he's since returned to racing and is doing well for himself).

On my return to the mainland, I went to Leeds to see Toby Branfoot – who bluntly told me that if I messed up this recovery there was a chance I could lose full use of my leg. He totally freaked me out, but it did me some good because I did exactly what I was told following the operation. That's not something I'm always very good at. Previously, after my accidents, I'd be desperate to get up and become active as quickly as possible. Just a week after they'd put something in my collarbone or my wrist, I'd be on the telephone asking whether I could go to the gym. This time I had to learn to walk again, so I took note of Toby's warning – which meant I was facing the prospect of many months without getting on a motorbike.

CHAPTER 16

A DOWNWARD SPIRAL

The physical injuries from the accident at the Manx were bad enough, but it was in my mind that I really suffered the consequences of that crash.

After leaving Sheffield, I'd returned to Northampton to live in a house that I shared with two other women and a guy. I hadn't felt a part of the house 'community' because I was away from it so often, testing or racing, and didn't have much of a chance to build up a relationship with the others, although they were friendly enough.

One of the other women living there was Michelle Rae, who had a very good job with the clothing company Levi's, but our paths rarely crossed – while I was off racing or testing she was regularly travelling to Belgium for her work.

However, while I was lying in hospital on the Isle of Man she telephoned to say that she'd read about the accident in a newspaper and to ask how I was. She seemed genuinely concerned for me and, during our long chat, I told her that I hoped to be out of a wheelchair and on crutches by the time I got back to Northampton. She said she'd do whatever she could to help me, and was as good as her word.

Without her, I'd have been trapped in my bedroom for most of the time. My mum would come over a couple of times a week to do what she could for me, help tidy my room and fuss over me, but Michelle ran around after me, cooking my dinners, getting me bits and pieces that I needed and helping me move about the house so I didn't feel so isolated. Once I could get about more easily, she would pack me into her car and take me shopping because I wasn't going to be driving for some while. She was brilliant, a fantastic help, and we became really good friends. So it was difficult for me when she moved back home to Scotland, where she has since had a baby.

That house quickly became impossible for me to live in. The landlady got rid of the tumble drier because she didn't like the size of the electricity bills, but that was only the start of her energy-saving craze. She took out most of the light bulbs from their sockets to save very little money, and not only turned the heating off but also took the fuse out of the heater in the front room. I tried to explain that I couldn't move about freely and I could only get out when someone like Michelle took me in her car; there was no way I could sit in the cold all day long, but she didn't want to hear it. What she didn't know was that I had this little electric fan heater in my bedroom and I had it switched on all the time, which must have cancelled out any savings she achieved through her crazy methods.

I knew it couldn't go on like that for too long. Her behaviour helped encourage me to get out and move up north with Dave, who had pretty much become my instant boyfriend following events on the Isle of Man. In the aftermath of the crash, he'd travel down from Preston on most weekends to stay with me in Northampton and he was brilliant through the tough times. So much so that we got engaged after I moved to be with him.

Unfortunately, I was having a tough time coming to terms with what had happened at the Manx. I'd spent too long in that bedroom, mulling over my life as a racer, and I began to question whether all the pain and disappointment was worth it. I asked myself if this was what I really wanted to do. Did I want to continue putting my body through all that battering? Wasn't my pledge to return to racing just a case of me trying to prove all over again how tough I was?

I got very down.

I had friends like Jayne and Michelle saying to me, "You'll carry on racing because it's what you love," but in the back of my mind, although I did still love the sport, I was saying to myself, *You know what? I'm not sure I want to do this anymore.* More and more I was asking myself whether the time had come to give up, whether I still had the passion and commitment that you need to put your life on the line each time you take to the start line.

When I moved to Preston with Dave, I enjoyed being with him but couldn't help worrying about whether our relationship would be affected if I went back to racing. Racing and relationships do not always mix, and it concerned me that I might have to decide which one got my full attention.

But biking had been my life, and even if I was having my

doubts I couldn't just turn my back on it. That autumn I went to the NEC Bike Show with Dave, an event I always enjoyed visiting as there were always plenty of familiar faces and I enjoyed finding out what the manufacturers were up to. I got talking to Paul Lindsay, the editor of *Irish Racing* magazine who also published the programme for the event, and he told me about a guy who was setting up a team and showing an interest in backing me.

So I met this guy and he seemed really keen. He was going on about how he'd have me racing at the TT, how he'd have me back in Superstock and how he had all these big plans for me. I stood there thinking, *I'm on crutches – has he actually had a proper look at me?* He was a good talker, a clever salesman, and there was a part of me that was tempted even though I was telling myself that I wasn't ready for all that yet, it simply wasn't possible or practical.

I think I really wanted to believe him, but I spoke to a couple of friends in the racing world and they were like, "Actually, Maria, we're not sure about him." I took their advice and told him I'd have to wait to see how my recovery went before I could make any definitive plans, but he was so pushy – he telephoned me up to five times a day, always asking the same question: "Have you decided yet?" I was like, *Wow, this is too much,* and eventually I told him I wasn't going with him, which was the right decision – he went with some other racers and ripped them off instead.

* * *

I became friendly with Derek Redmond, an athlete who'd also gone to school in Northamptonshire and went on to win gold medals at the World Championships, European Championships and Commonwealth Games. You'll probably remember him from the 1992 Olympic Games in Barcelona, when he tore his hamstring in the semi-finals of the 400 metres but, propped up by his dad, still managed to complete his lap and receive a standing ovation as he hobbled down the final straight.

Derek was very much into his psychology and once told me that, at the start of an Olympic final, all the runners lining up are capable of winning that race. They've all got to that peak physical state and done everything they possibly can to prepare themselves – it all comes down to who is in the strongest state of mind.

That's absolutely true. If your mind is not in the right place then you're not going to be able to compete effectively. I knew that was going to be a big problem for me if I was going to return to racing; I had too many doubts to do the job properly.

Dave really enjoyed his racing – he was a good pal of Alan and Andy Jackson – and he was very supportive of me. He was a good sounding board, but I began to feel quite isolated up there in Preston. I wasn't seeing friends and family, people I cared about, as much as I should, and I knew I wasn't as happy as I should have been. With my future as a racer continually in doubt, I ended up going to see a doctor who prescribed antidepressants.

I did want it to work with Dave, who's a smashing guy. But, as the racers began gearing up for the 2007 season I drifted back towards the sport, largely because I couldn't see any real alternative.

Having had no time or inclination to look around for a team, I went racing on my own but really wasn't up to it. I'd persevered with my physiotherapy and gym work over the winter because I wanted to be in the best possible physical shape, regardless of what my future held. By the summer I told myself I was fit enough to race, and perhaps I could do the Manx again.

But I quickly discovered that, even though I'd convinced myself I could race, I was having to face up to something I hadn't encountered before – a little bit of fear. It wasn't so much that I was afraid of getting physically busted up again, although I wasn't overly keen on the prospect. It was more a case of spates of panic, along the lines of *Oh my God, if I haven't got racing what have I got?*

Because I was living in Lancashire, I decided to enter a race at Oulton Park. I had a new sponsor who lent me his motorhome for the weekend and Dave came with me, but I simply couldn't go fast enough. I'd go out for practice, ride poorly and return to the paddock in tears. I was very hard on myself, saying I wasn't going out again, and though I'm normally able to draw strength from those around me – which is why I need good people in my team – this time it didn't matter what anybody else said. It wasn't sinking in.

What I should have done was give myself some breathing space and afford my body and mind time to rebuild themselves after the physical and mental trauma of the Manx crash. Instead, I was forcing myself to go out on the bike and compete when I didn't feel up to it – a very dangerous state of affairs for a biker.

This was one of those times when I'm my own worst enemy, destroying myself with my contradictions and self-doubt. On the one hand I'd encountered fear for the first time and didn't feel up to racing; yet, on the other, I couldn't stop myself from worrying about what other people would think of me if I 'chickened out'. I decided I needed help and started seeing the sports psychologist Brian Hemmings, who said my problems ran deeper than just my chosen sport and recommended a more personal type of counselling. This helped me work through a number of issues and I began to realise that I needed to bring balance to my life.

I loved my racing, but I'd been moving up and down the country for the past decade, never staying in the same place for too long. Even though I normally had a lot of people around me, I'd cut myself off from some of those I cared about. I realised I had some great mates – people like Jayne, Michelle and Debbie – yet I didn't always pay heed to the fact that they were there for me. Because I'd been off here, there and everywhere, I'd built up this circle of friends I could come back to after a six-month absence and chat to as if it were yesterday. But now I decided I needed to start seeing more of them.

For years I'd focused on the racing, it had been number one in my life, but perhaps I'd used it as an excuse to not deal with the things I'm not so good at. There were times when I needed to put more of an effort into my personal life, but I'd hide behind the excuse that I was too busy to be distracted. And so situations that should have been sorted tended to drag on, to the dissatisfaction of all concerned.

With Dave it was never just a case of making the simple

choice 'biking or boyfriend', but I did have my doubts about quite how suited we were. So I called off the engagement and decided to move back to Northampton – although, unfortunately, I quickly got myself involved with another guy who did a lot of damage to my fragile state of mind.

CHAPTER 17

HOLLYWOOD HERE I COME!

Dave Jefferies said to me in 2002, "You're going to be really jealous of me – I'm going to be on a PlayStation game." Here was an absolute legend of the motorcycling world, an amazing racer who had won the British Superstock Championship, the fastest man ever at the Isle of Man with God knows how many TT titles under his belt, and he seemed more excited about being featured on a computer game than everything else he'd achieved put together!

He was telling me how Jester, a company which makes computer games, had been photographing his bike and leathers and how he was going to be immortalised in a game called *TT Superbikes*. I wasn't jealous, but I did think to myself how nice it would be to be recognised like that – and then I found out I was to be part of the game too!

Of the 50 riders used by Jester, I was the only woman. I didn't say much to people about it at the time because I think I was afraid somebody would sneer that I was only the token female. But, like Dave, I did find it more exciting than I probably should have done. Once it was released I got quite a lot of attention from people who'd never been anywhere near a race track. It made me feel quite cool!

It had all come about when I went to a Steve Hislop memorial day at Cadwell Park, a circuit sometimes affectionately referred to as 'the mini Nurburgring', after the famous German track. The day was being run by Stamford Superbikes, a bike shop which had made an approach to me about potential sponsorship, and the plan was for me to ride on one of Dave's old race bikes, something I felt honoured to be doing.

We were put up in a hotel near the circuit and we all went out for a meal on the evening before the track day. There were all sorts of different people there and I happened to sit next to a guy called Clark Evans, a director of Jester. We got talking and Clark said, "We're definitely having you on the game as well." I was like, *Yes!* It was hard to stop myself smiling!

Not that I had to do much. Jester took photographs of my bikes and leathers and married them up to the computer-generated images they used. The included me in both versions of the PlayStation2 game – in the first I'm on the Suzuki 750 that I set my Isle of Man lap record on, while for the later version I ride a Bering Honda 600.

The game was released in 2004. Shortly afterwards, I was at a race meeting chatting to a man who had his two young daughters with him. "Tell them who you were the other day," he said to the eldest. "I was Maria Costello," she said. Then the younger girl chipped in, "I was Maria Costello as well!" So, there you have it – I was immortalised! I was given a copy of the game and I'm crap at it, but I did laugh when the girls told me how they were racing Maria Costello against Maria Costello – that's one way of making sure I win. Plus you have to get to a certain level before you can even become me!

From a financial point of view, this sort of thing is a great way of keeping my sponsors happy. I used it as another opportunity to tap up a few more backers on the promise that they'd be promoted in virtual reality, as well as real life. Anything that makes you stand out from the crowd is an advantage when you're chasing money, and the response to the game was good.

Jester sent out a press release saying they were delighted to include me as a featured rider. From now on, whenever I got asked what it was like for a girl to race around the TT course, I could tell people to go try it out for themselves!

I also found my way into a television drama, although in the first instance it had little to do with me being a bike racer. I'd already done a fair amount of TV work for the likes of Men & Motors and Anglia, and I'd also got involved with Sporting Champions, which uses sportsmen and women to encourage youngsters into a more active lifestyle as part of a government-funded PE and sports scheme.

I was at one of their functions when I got talking to this guy who was part of a BMX extreme team. I was telling him how much I loved my mountain bike and how it helped keep me fit for motorbike racing, nothing more than casual conversation, but a few weeks later the same guy called me up and said he'd been asked to double in an ITV drama, *Walk Away and I Stumble*, that was about to start filming. They also needed a girl – so would I be interested? He told me all I'd have to do was ride up and down a few hills in Hampshire.

It sounded like fun, so I agreed and set off for the location at some ungodly hour of the morning. It was near Andover, which was doubling as Stonehenge for the purpose of the drama, where I met the director, the stunt coordinator and a stunt girl. I was told that all I'd have to do was ride my bike downhill and, although there would be a tumble off the bike, the stunt girl would be taking over from me for that bit. How hard could it be?

I was taken off to where I was supposed to do my bit – and I couldn't believe my eyes. I looked down this hill that I was supposed to ride down and it wasn't so much a hill as a complete drop-off – it was pretty much a natural version of the half-pipes they use in extreme gravity sports, and it was absolutely massive.

It was way out of my league, I'd never ridden on anything like it, and I sat on my bike thinking, *I can't do this – what have I let myself in for?* Mike, the BMX guy, was saying things like, "This is a piece of cake," and "We'll do this, no trouble." I was sitting there thinking, *I'm totally out of my depth here – what do I do?* It was alright for Mike, he was an extreme BMXer; I was just a girl who liked to ride her bike.

To make matters worse, the director got a bit excited and started telling us how he wanted us flying up ramps and doing these big jumps. With every sentence he spoke he seemed to come up with yet another daft idea. When he said, "I'll need to see you crossing in the air," I felt the blood drain out of my face. I wondered how I should break the news to him that I just wasn't going to be able to do it.

Fortunately, the stunt coordinator piped up and told him,

"No, that's not actually possible." I was quietly gripping the handlebars, trying to look in control, but giving him a very appreciative round of applause in my head! The director was out to create some fairy story, but all I knew was that he wasn't going to get any help from me.

They eventually agreed on what the stunt coordinator insisted was practical, and then announced that filming was to start – I wasn't even going to get a dry run at it! I'd already been put into costume – the wig and makeup were no problem, but they stuck me in these wedge high-heels which were sellotaped to my feet so I wouldn't lose them as I tried to ride the bike down the slope. "Why am I wearing these shoes when I'm on a push bike?" I asked. Their sarcastic reply let me know that doubles were simply meant to be seen and not heard.

Fortunately, the stunt girl who was taking over the end-of-ride fall, assuming I got that far, was lovely. She was far more aware than the director of what was being demanded of me, and asked if I had any protection. Of course I hadn't, so she gave me some pads for my elbows and knees, which I was able to hide away under my costume (a tight shirt and three-quarter length shorts).

I was doubling for Tamzin Outhwaite, an actress who'd become famous for her role as Melanie Owen in *EastEnders* for four years up until 2002. Her character was supposed to be a guide at Stonehenge who apparently suffered from frequent blackouts; some guy was to turn up at Stonehenge on his mountain bike and they'd go off and do stuff together – it was all a bit odd.

She wasn't at the location while I was doing my bit. I'd taken my own mountain bike along and they were happy to let me use it, which I'd initially thought was a good idea (before quickly finding out that it wasn't). I had no choice but to go for it, so I went over the edge and almost immediately lost control of the bike. I was thrown off and landed in a pile of sheep shit. I'd torn the costume, I was covered in poo and I just lay there feeling like I really didn't want to get up – I was being paid to be a stunt double but I couldn't do it.

One of the wardrobe ladies came rushing down the hill in a panic. "Oh my God, we've only got one more shirt – you won't be coming off again, will you?" she asked as I picked myself up. "No, of course not," I said, without believing a word of it.

As they were stripping off the poo-stained clothing and trying to re-dress me, my sister rang to moan about the mare of a day she was supposedly having. I snapped back that it couldn't be as bad as mine. "I'm supposed to be a double for one of England's top actresses and I'm standing at the bottom of one of the steepest hills I've ever seen, covered in sheep shit! And I can't do what they want me to do," I added, close to tears. Suddenly, Tina's problems weren't quite so important. "All you've got to do is keep telling yourself you're a stuntwoman," she told me. I hung up the phone, quietly whispering to myself over and over, *I'm a stuntwoman, I can do this.*

And I did! I got the stunt people to alter the height of the seat on my mountain bike, which had been too high for going down the hill, and set off again, this time making it all the way to the bottom without a scratch – I don't know who was the most relieved, me or the wardrobe lady! I then stood watching as the stunt girl wandered over to take a small fall (the Tamzin Outhwaite character was supposed to have a blackout) and said to myself, *That was the easy part – I could have done that.*

A short while later, this stunt girl was asked to double for Reese Witherspoon for a remake of the modern-day fairytale *Penelope*, the original of which was released in 1966 with Natalie Wood in the leading role. The film was a sort of loose social commentary about a well-bred and wealthy young woman who'd be an ideal date for any young man – except for the fact that her face was supposed to resemble that of a pig.

Christina Ricci played the lead character with Reese, whose production company Type A was making the film, taking a secondary role as Annie, best friend of the cursed Penelope. Part of the film was set in London and Reese's character was supposed to buzz around the streets on a moped, but the stunt girl couldn't do the riding because she didn't have a road licence. Remembering me from my poo-stained dramatics in *Walk Away and I Stumble*, she told Reese that she knew a girl who could, and so, out of the blue, I got a call from the film's stunt director asking me if I'd like a few days' work.

In the light of my previous experience, I wanted to know exactly what was expected this time. "It's only a bit of light riding, easy, no problem," he said. He also explained that he'd been told I had blonde hair, but needed a picture of me to make sure I could double for Reese who, as the producer, would have to approve me. "And you definitely can ride a motorbike, can't you?" he asked me. "You have definitely got a licence to ride on the road?" I told him to take a look at my website, as it had everything on there that he needed to know. (After a short while he rang back to say, "I'm so embarrassed.")

He told me that the job they required me for was a walk in the park for someone of my biking pedigree. And the money was brilliant. As they'd struggled to find someone to do the riding so close to the filming date, the stunt guy told me I could call the shots. I ended up earning my normal three months' wages in three days, with all my expenses paid. I spent three days in London at different venues and was even given my own trailer with my name on the door!

Obviously I had to get in costume again, and they added some little bits to my hair because Reese had plaits for her part. She was tiny and, although I'm petite, I felt huge compared to her. We only met briefly because, when it was her time to be on set, she arrived in an enormous blacked-out Range Rover with four bouncers who were all gigantic. She was already in costume and did no more than step out of the car, sit on her bike, say her two lines and then get straight back into the car to be driven off.

Christina Ricci was much more sociable and often hung around with the rest of the cast and crew. At one of the venues, we were waiting in a pub for everything to be set up and she was chatting away. With her being such a big name in cinema, having been an actress since starring in *The Addams Family* as a little girl, I was a little bit in awe of her at first but soon realised she was just like any other girl. *Actually, you're pretty normal,* I thought as she talked about getting her nails done and going shopping, which wasn't a conversation I could get too interested in.

I was quite nervous to start with, but it was as easy as the stunt coordinator had told me it would be. All I had to do was ride a Vesper scooter. The girl doubling for Christina was a great laugh, while all the people I was working with – the director and assistant director, cameramen, sound guy and boom guy – all knew I had a history of racing at the TT. They'd found these twisty little roads and had them blocked off so I could do my bit. One of the cameramen said, "I'm going to be lying on the floor right next to the kerb and I need you to come as close to the camera as you can, as fast as you can."

So I went at him full pelt and flew by within an inch of him. The rest of the crew fell about laughing as the cameraman stood up and said, "Okay, I don't need you to go that fast – or come that close!" I finished where they'd put a mark on the road, then went and sat out of shot while Reese and Christina did their bit. Then I'd be called back for the next bit of riding, which was never anything more dramatic than a gentle scoot along the road.

As with the TV drama, I had my problems with one of the wardrobe ladies. Reese's character was a courier girl and, in one of the scenes on the bike, she was supposed to ride along with a satchel over her shoulder. They only had the one satchel, so whenever she turned up for her lines it got taken off me, put on her, and then it'd come back to me when she'd finished.

But, for one take, I somehow ended up riding without the satchel on me. When that terrible fact was discovered it was like the end of the world. I felt like I'd murdered somebody. This woman was going ballistic at me, shouting, "Why didn't you put the satchel on?" and stabbing her fingers at other members of the crew, screaming over and over, "Why didn't you put the satchel on her?" I stood there thinking, *Oh my God, I've ruined the film!* The wardrobe woman got even more worked up when somebody told her they couldn't re-shoot because Christina, who was in the scene with me, had disappeared. The shot they eventually used was less than a second long, and you'd need Superman-style vision to be able to spot the fact that there was no satchel on the rider.

On the first day of filming, the plan was for me to take Christina on the back of the scooter. Unfortunately, perhaps because I was a little nervous, there was a misunderstanding at the moment she was supposed to climb onto the back. As she went to sit down I accelerated off, leaving her standing legs apart in the road. How embarrassing! I had to go back to do a second take, and this time we made our short ride together. Christina seemed to take it in good spirits but she didn't get on the bike again – thereafter, whenever there was any riding to be done, it was always her double.

Because of her part, Reese's character had to wear an oversized helmet and huge goggles; as I was standing in for her I had to do likewise. We were filming at the time when that totally annoying Crazy Frog song was being played on the radio, and *The Sun* ran a picture of Reese with her helmet and goggles on, comparing her to the Crazy Frog character. I read the paper thinking, *If she looks like him then I must do too.*

For one scene, filmed in the centre of London, I had to ride along a narrow road and move out of shot around a corner. As I turned, I was greeted by a wall of paparazzi photographers. So many flashes went off at the same time that I had trouble seeing for a few minutes afterwards. As you might expect, they weren't there for me but were hoping to get some pictures of Christina Ricci with her face done up like a pig. (I got talking to a few of the photographers and asked if they could send me copies of their pictures, which they did.)

I also spent some time with the guy whose job it was to make the prosthetic nose for Christina's character, and it was interesting to see how he modelled it from different materials and shaped it for the actress, matching her skin tone. I also spent time in makeup with Richard E. Grant, who was lovely, very chatty and friendly, and, for some strange reason, at meal times I got to eat first with all the stars – apparently, that's a perk of being a double. All the extras got stuck on a double decker bus and were given the scraps, but I got fantastic roast dinners and other amazing food – I could even have had it delivered to my trailer if I'd asked, although I didn't have the ego for that!

When the movie trailers were shown to promote the film, it featured a little bit of me on the scooter. I really thought I'd made it. But when the film came out there wasn't much more of me in it than had featured in the trailer! Then I got asked to do some stunt work for the film *Tomb Raider II*, which had Angelina Jolie in the lead role as Lara Croft. I was really excited about doing that but, before filming was due to start in London, I broke my wrist racing at Silverstone and was forced to miss out, which was a huge disappointment.

I've also done my share of television work, and a documentary by Anglia TV was very much an eye opener for me. They came to the Isle of Man and filmed not only me, but also my family back home in Spratton. They then showed us what they'd been filming; my parents got to see me doing what I love to do, while I got to see how worried they get when I go off to race. My dad was nearly in tears when I set off, saying, "We're really sad to see her go," while my mum claimed, "We're very proud of her." Which wasn't what they were saying to me at the time!

Anglia asked my dad if I'd broken many bones, and he said, "Yeah, she's broken her leg a few times," which I hadn't at the time – that was to come later. However, I can understand the confusion, because by then I had broken so many bones – including my pelvis and ankle – that I think they'd given up counting. There was a bit in the documentary where I was being cheeky with Neil Hodgson, who had won the 2000 British Superbike Championship and the 2003 Superbike World Championship titles before going off to the United States to ride in the American Superbike Championship. When the programme was shown on television I got accused of chatting him up. But so what if I did? He's a really good looking guy and he's fast on a motorbike, so what girl wouldn't have taken that opportunity?

Another programme I appeared in was about the unsung heroes of the TT races, and I was selected as one of the four featured riders. This was put together in the year that DJ was killed and they've got a great bit of footage of me and him chatting. I'm so glad the TV cameras caught us larking about, because now I have a snippet of how he used to be with me: not that I could ever forget. On this occasion we were in the TT paddock and he was playing up to the cameras, emphasising how easy it was to wind me up – standing behind me and motioning as if he was turning a key in my back. It's brilliant, and every time I watch it I end up in tears. They also worked into the programme a memorial piece about DJ, which is very sad to watch.

There was a spell when I was on television so much that I'd go into Tesco and people would come up and say, "You're Maria Costello!" I did a Granada TV programme called *Fran's Angels* in which I went to the Isle of Man to interview Neil Hodgson, which I enjoyed for obvious reasons. I also got to interview US GP winner Nicky Hayden, having missed two previous appointments with him – something that he reminded me about as soon as he saw me! I had to wait for him to come out of a long meeting with some top bods from Honda and, while I was waiting, I bumped into Gavan Caldwell, a great photographer from Ireland. (Check out his site, *www.bikesportireland.com.*)

Gavan hung around with me and, when Nicky finally appeared out of the race truck (it was well worth the wait), he got some great pictures of me interviewing Nicky alongside his GP bike in his garage. Apparently, I was grinning like a Cheshire cat throughout the entire interview – I can't think why! – and Gavan got it all on film.

I also took part in a Men & Motors panel show targeted at bikers, while one of the more rewarding bits of television work I got involved in was for the Discovery Channel. They had plans for this programme which they called *Big, Big Bikes* and they got me to race my bike against a car. It was snowing that morning and I began to doubt whether the race would go ahead, but it did eventually and, by the time they had us on the start line, I was desperate to beat the guy. I can't remember his name, but he'd won at Daytona or something and seemed completely up himself.

Prior to the race, we'd been filmed separately with both of us asked pretty much the same questions. They said to me, "Do you think you're going to win?" and I said that of course I was, as we were going in a straight line and I was on a motorbike, while he was only in a Porsche. Then they asked him and he started droning on and on about all his experience, and how he really knew how to race. I normally manage to get on with most people, but this guy wound me up so much that I wanted to put him in his place.

On arriving at the venue, I'd seen the snow and told myself to take it steady because I knew the runway would be slippery. I also had a sore back that meant I couldn't sit comfortably on the bike but, after being wound up by this guy, I really wanted to rub his nose in the dirt. We set off from a standing start and I immediately accelerated clear of him, increasing my lead the further we went. If you watch the programme, you'll see they have a camera at the finish line and I finish so far ahead of him that he should be embarrassed by it. Vicky Butler Henderson, who's the commentator, says, "Here comes the bike ... one [long pause] ... two [long pause] ... three [long pause] ... we've got the car."

I enjoyed that moment. When I'm doing my talks for Sporting Champions or the Women's Sports Foundation, or visiting a school, I often show that clip because it's good for the younger generation to see the girl beating the guy.

CHAPTER 18

RELATIONSHIPS ARE THE KILLER

Just as an ugly-mug man can seem a whole lot sexier once he starts racing a motorbike, the way in which many men look at me is definitely different because I'm a biker. There was a stage in my life when I actually wouldn't tell any man I got chatting to that I was a racer. To some it seemed to be the sexiest thing they'd ever heard and that's all they'd want to talk about, while others obviously didn't believe me.

Either way, it was difficult to get a decent conversation going. So if I was out in a bar or club and I wasn't in the mood to talk bikes, then I'd just make up something else. Sometimes I'd assume the identity of a friend of mine and pretend that I made Levi's for a living or that I was a veterinary nurse. I wasn't being impolite or condescending, but I spend so much of my life surrounded by bikers that it's nice sometimes to go out and not talk about racing or bikes or circuits.

Because I was such a slow starter with the opposite sex, I didn't really get into relationships until I'd already become involved in racing. Almost my entire adult life has revolved around bikes, and this is how I've met most of the guys I've dated.

I don't have a week and a weekend like lots of other people, I don't go to work for five days and then have two days to go to the pub. In fact, I don't go out regularly and I don't really drink. When most people are out on a Friday or Saturday night, I'm often at a race meeting, or testing somewhere, or working on my PR. It's a sacrifice that I've had to make, though I'm not really into alcohol anyway – I used to drink more when I was younger, but I now do so much training to keep in shape that I wouldn't want to spoil it.

I certainly don't feel as if I've missed out because of the choices I've made. I get to do exactly what I want to do, I meet amazing people and I've been to some wonderful places that I'd never have got the chance to see without racing. There's also a great social side to racing, and there's always a party or gathering at each meeting. I enjoy myself at some of these when I get the chance to get off my bike and relax, although nowadays I generally steer clear of alcohol. At the Isle of Man, the saying is 'Looking forward to the beer tent at the end of the week.' When you go to somewhere like the North West 200 or Goodwood there are some great social occasions as well.

We live in a funny old world in which those who don't drink are almost looked down on as an oddity. I find that, when I'm in a nightclub or at a party, some people can't accept that I don't want to drink alcohol. This is how the conversation inevitably goes: "Why don't you drink?"; then it's, "Go on, have a drink; you can have *one* drink"; then they're almost forcing it on me.

Of course, many of the old-school racers were party animals and there was a time when the two went hand in hand. You'd ride hard and fast during the day and then party even harder through the night, getting back on your bike the next day to go even faster with a hangover! I always used to think, *Flipping hell, that's not fair – how do they do it?* I never thought I could race like that, although at the Goodwood Revival in 2009 I did drink a little the night before racing, simply because the champagne was so nice – then, the next morning, I got up and went two seconds quicker than I had the day before. I was telling everybody that I should drink champagne more often!

But I've learned that it's possible not to drink and still to have a good time. Particularly as I'm female and I'm on my own, sometimes it's better to have my wits about me. I say that because, one evening I was at an event in Assen, Holland, there was a massive party on the Sunday evening to round off the event. I'm such a lightweight that I'll be drunk after two drinks anyway, but this one evening I'd had a few more than that, and I didn't really have much of a clue what was happening when I was dragged off on the back of some guy's scooter. Thankfully, one of the English racers, a great guy by the name of Andy Notman, saw what was happening, came over and pulled me off, telling the guy, "She doesn't want to go with you."

Who knows what would have happened? Perhaps nothing more than a spin around the track, but it did make me realise how vulnerable I can be. And I've always liked Andy – he used to do European Superstock when I worked for a world

Supersport team, so we used to hang out but he never came on to me and we became really good friends.

There have been periods in my life when I've got so into my racing that I've found myself getting too cut off from everything else, too isolated. I'd get really serious about training and lose contact with my family and friends; it was never intentional, it just happened that way. For years and years I put motorbiking at number one and let everything else suffer. If things started to go wrong with a boyfriend, I could always tell myself, *Oh well, I'm concentrating on my racing,* so I didn't have to think too deeply about the reasons why. When your self-image is as poor as mine then it's a less painful escape route.

Some guys are attracted to me because they have this perception of me as a tough female, different to a lot of the girls they come into contact with. Yet as soon as I show them my softer, more vulnerable side, they'll be saying things like, "Oh, I wasn't expecting that – you're just like all the other women." And I'll think to myself, *I don't* want *to be soft, but that's the way I am. If you can't handle that then perhaps you should go out and find somebody who* is *tougher than me.*

A former boyfriend, who did me a lot of damage when my self-esteem was really low in 2008, kept saying to me, "I didn't think you were like this." So one day I asked him whether this was a bad thing. He replied, "No, no, no, it's just different to what I expected," which I saw as a bad sign because he obviously wanted to go out with the image, not the real me.

Because of the glamour that many people perceive in the sport, a lot of guys think I'm going to be really outgoing, loud and full of myself; they think that I'm rich, a bit of a celebrity and that I'll have some kind of aura about me. After I'd been out on a few dates with one guy, he admitted that he'd been expecting to date a woman who was a bit more arrogant. When you go through these kinds of experiences, it can make you suspicious of men. Plus I'm too much of a thinker: I'm always trying to work out the whys and wherefores of why somebody would want me.

Chris Moss, my first proper boyfriend, did me a lot of damage and it took me several years to get over him. I was very young and inexperienced with regard to men when we got together, and I didn't have much idea of what relationships are all about. I also have a fear of rejection, which is something I can't help, but it's a downside to relationships. There are times when I know when a guy is no good for me and that I should let go, but I keep hanging on, finding it so difficult to make the final break even though it's the only logical and sensible step.

After I found out that Chris had cheated on me I should have walked away, but I didn't. He was good at playing mind games while I was quite naïve, and it wasn't long before it was *me* who was feeling guilty about the fact that he'd felt it necessary to go to South Africa and sleep with a hotel maid. Instead of insisting on the inevitable break, I kept trying to patch things up, talk things through, make a fresh start ... we acted out just about every cliché in the book. It got horrible and I ended up being prescribed antidepressants by a doctor.

I get on well with Chris now. We'll share a laugh and a joke when we bump into each other, and he's a smooth talker. I saw him at Silverstone in the summer of 2009 and he was still at it, saying to me, "Why didn't you look this good when we were going out?"

And there were some good things which came out of our relationship – especially when, following his crash at the TT, I was invited to stay at the home of my absolute hero, Steve Hislop. He came to visit Chris in hospital and, when I told him I didn't want to go home and leave Chris, Steve offered me the chance to stay with him and his girlfriend Kelly. As well as adoring him as a racing legend, I'd had a secret crush on Steve for many years, so to stay in his house on the island was amazing. When I first got into bikes I'd asked for his autograph loads of times, and suddenly here I was, having a beer and watching television with him in his home, and talking about bike racing. One day he took me up to his loft, which was like a Steve Hislop museum – full of all his old leathers, his first helmet, photographs, magazine articles and trophies. As I walked around the room I was pinching myself, I felt so privileged.

I stayed with Steve and Kelly for a week before Chris was flown back in a private plane to hospital in Leicester, near his home. My mum and dad would drive up from Spratton to help look after him, doing some of the cleaning, gardening and running around for him. With Chris unable to work, I managed to pick up a few of his road tests for *Motorcycle News*.

I can't say I learned from what happened with Chris and I was quickly onto the next bloke, Shaun Hawker, who worked for *Classic Bike Magazine*. That didn't last long and it was the start of a handful of relationships in which my self-doubt would become a negative influence. I'd go out with a guy for a while, probably get too involved too quickly, and then start telling myself I wasn't good enough for him; I'd talk myself out of it and the relationship would fizzle out. I do fall in love too easily – although perhaps I shouldn't use the 'L' word, as I'm not sure I really know what it means.

I'm always trying to work out the ulterior motive of any guy I start seeing: *What are you doing here? Why do you like me?* It probably doesn't help that most of the guys I meet are involved in racing in some way, even if only as a fan. I don't go out on the town every Saturday to meet guys like a lot of girls do, and with my lifestyle I'm not likely to meet anybody in a conventional way. Because we're doing the same sort of thing, it's easy to get talking; we'll probably have a certain knowledge about each other already, and even if the other guy isn't a racer he'll think he knows me. I'll invariably be told, "It's great being able to talk about motorbikes to a girl," "It's amazing that you ride motorbikes," or, "It's so easy to talk to you." They must think they're the first person to say it to me, but they're not.

When a relationship does start to make progress, it always has to compete with the racing or the consequences of my accidents. My relationship with Darren was doomed from the moment I had one of my crashes – he just wasn't able to support somebody struggling to cope with pretty big physical and mental consequences. Dave, too, was a really nice guy who I probably met at the wrong time in my life.

But I never seem to learn from my mistakes, and probably the most destructive relationship was with a guy I got involved with after calling off my engagement to Dave. I'd returned to Northampton because I wanted to concentrate on just being myself, being single, building myself up again after that last accident and spending more time with friends. I seemed to be getting my life in some sort of order; even if I was still in a bit of turmoil over racing, I was doing PR for Bering and a few other bits and pieces to keep me busy and occupied. Then I met Dominic, once again through racing.

Of course, I shouldn't have got involved with him as quickly as I did. But that's me. After being so determined to lead an independent life and put myself and my friends ahead of everything else, I found myself part of a couple again. As with pretty much every guy I've been involved with, Dominic's roots were firmly planted in motorcycle racing. A decade before we got together we'd raced in the CB 500 Cup against each other – although our paths never really crossed and I can't pretend that I knew him.

But while I was in Northampton, trying to rebuild my confidence and decide whether I had it in me to return to racing, I was offered a free track day in Spain. Dominic, who was organising a group of people to take to the event, was a mutual friend of the person who invited me, so we made contact through Facebook and it started from there – I blame him for the addiction to Facebook that I've had ever since!

We got on so well from the word go that I couldn't seem to stop myself getting involved with him, even though my friends were urging caution. As we were going through that stage of finding out everything about each other, I opened up to him about the doubts I had because of my injury and how

I was troubled by what the future held. He was totally reassuring in those early weeks; he was lovely, in fact, but after we moved into a rented house in Brixworth, a few miles north of Northampton, he became bored by making the effort and our relationship, still only a few months old, went downhill very quickly.

I don't think there was any one obvious incident that started the rot, but I became very insecure very quickly about the way things were between us, and he was really good at playing on those insecurities. He began to distance himself from me and started going out in the evening without me. When I challenged him about it, he said, "I just can't reassure you anymore. I've given you all the reassurance I can give – you've got to get yourself sorted out."

What I should have done was take note of his change in attitude and finish the relationship before he could inflict any damage on me. I knew in my heart there was no future in it. But my inherent insecurity meant that, once again, I couldn't let go of a doomed relationship. Things just got worse and worse and I reached a point where I was upset all the time; I didn't want to get out of bed; I didn't want to leave the house. I went off my food and began losing the weight I'd put back on; I felt so unhappy but I couldn't find the motivation to do anything about it.

But something about him had really hooked me and, despite all the pain and unhappiness the relationship was causing, I couldn't let go. We'd go days without talking and when we did we'd only argue, leaving me feeling even worse than I already was.

Some of Dominic's friends were not a good influence on him either and seemed to take an instant dislike to me, causing him to feel torn. I never wanted to be part of a crowd that I didn't like or trust, but Dominic either couldn't or didn't want to give them up. It got to the stage where the only way I knew what he was up to was by reading about it on Facebook.

I knew how ridiculous it was. There was no point to our relationship and things were only going to get worse. But I ran away from making a decision. One day we'd agree to separate and the next day we'd make up.

I've still got a text message he sent me on the day when we really did hit rock bottom. I'd sent him a text earlier to say I was feeling really low and asking him to give me a ring – he sent a reply back saying *he* was feeling really low so why didn't *I* ring him? Arguing by text or Facebook or email is so much more confrontational than face to face; there's less room for compromise and opinions polarise with each message. After he had sniped at me, I sent him a text asking if he was envious of me. It must have been the wrong question to ask him, because what I got back was a four-page text that seemed designed to destroy me.

It said: "why would I be jealous of you, you are nothing, you've achieved nothing, you dine out on your TT lap record, nobody likes you" ... it went on and on. I thought, *Wow, this is the guy who I love and who is supposed to love me.* Yet it did me a favour because it made me realise I simply had to break free – if I didn't, he was going to drag me down and drown me.

I finally got out when one evening, alone and depressed, I

sent a text to a lot of my friends saying that I was looking for a place to lodge. My good mate Roo rang me up from Sheffield and we had a long chat, I was telling him how bad I felt and what this particular relationship was doing to me. Roo told me about a friend of his who had a job working in Austria for the winter as a snowboard instructor, and said he'd arrange for me to go and stay with him. "Have a holiday, chill out, have a good time," was his instruction. He put us in touch and I liked the sound of this guy, so I made plans to travel to Austria for the Christmas holiday period.

I had a great time that Christmas. I have my own snowboard, I enjoy the thrill of the sport and it was great to be away from all the stress that had impacted on just about every aspect of my life over those previous months. As far as I was concerned, my relationship with Dominic was over. Yet, when I arrived back at the airport, I saw him waiting for me with a massive bouquet of flowers.

So, once again, a relationship that was inevitably doomed continued well past its sell-by date. It would even have a negative impact on my racing.

CHAPTER 19

THE YEARS OF DOUBT

Although I'd had a difficult time with Dominic, he wasn't my only problem during 2008. As I'd tried to rebuild my mental and physical confidence following the injuries I suffered at the Manx in 2006, I'd only rode competitively twice in the whole of 2007 and then, early into the 2008 season, my racing was again disrupted by yet another broken collarbone. Nothing unusual in that, you might think – but it came at a time when I was finding it so much more difficult to put my injuries behind me.

It was at the beginning of 2007 that I'd started having serious doubts for the first time about whether I wanted to continue racing. I was still suffering the after effects of the Manx and, although I'd a good boyfriend at the time in Dave – who tried everything to lift my morale and confidence, bless him – I just couldn't get my head together. When it was time for me to go out on my bike, I'd be in tears because I would be nervous and apprehensive, even a little afraid for the first time in my life. When I'd come back in I'd start bawling my eyes out, even if the ride had gone without incident. I remember thinking to myself, *Why am I doing this?* and the only answer I could come up with was, *Because this is what I do.*

I've got a lot of pride and I never want to be seen giving up, so I carried on with the physical recovery work during 2007. Although I'd had my doubts, I think I knew in the back of my mind that I'd have to carry on racing. By now I was approaching my 34th birthday, I'd been racing since my early twenties and I didn't know a lot else. I felt I belonged in the paddock, even if what I was going through on the track wasn't exactly producing a feel-good factor.

I needed to get that first race back under my belt if I was going to shake off the demons, and I decided that somewhere completely different might just do the job. So I sent off my entry for the Cock 'o' the North road races at Oliver's Mount in Scarborough, which is England's only remaining natural road circuit. While the other road circuits in England have gradually vanished from the racing calendar, Oliver's Mount has survived despite fixture clashes and loss of championship status basically because a lot of riders continued to support the venue.

I hadn't ridden the course but I'd heard plenty about it and thought it would be something fresh, with no memories to distract me. I went out on a Bering Honda RVF400 and surprised myself with how well it went, at least for a while. I was in seventh place when I was forced to retire because of a mechanical failure. But at least I'd survived my return to racing without too much mishap and it did make me feel a little better about myself.

Of course, a few laps at a solitary meeting, however encouraging, was not going to restore my confidence to where it was before the Manx in 2006. But going back to racing wasn't as scary as I'd led myself to believe it might be. So I decided I'd put in my entry for the Manx a month later, and, because I'd raced so little that summer, I thought I'd be able to go to the Isle of Man without any burden of expectation and, hopefully, get back my appetite for riding on the big stage.

I put my name down for both the junior and Ultra Lightweight races and took both my Bering Honda CBR600RR and Bering RVF400 with me. But I didn't feel good from the moment I arrived. I remember questioning myself as to why I'd taken two bikes with me. Why was I making things so hard for myself? I should have just taken the one bike, the 400, and set myself up for that. But it seemed that, just as I never want to be seen to give up, so I never want anybody to look at me and think I'm taking the easy way out. There have been too many times when I've got caught up in thinking that people were watching what I was doing and I couldn't let them see me as weak, so I'd try to act like this tough racer when, actually, I was feeling more vulnerable than they could ever imagine.

I'm sure there are guys who feel the same way, but perhaps because women are put down as the weaker sex – nowhere more so than in racing – I try too hard to prove my point. Yet the 'I wonder what people think of me?' scenario too often works against you, as I've demonstrated by trying to get back on a bike when I've not been well enough in body and mind, or forcing myself to continue riding in weather conditions when my instincts told me it would be prudent to stop.

Most people probably aren't watching, or are so busy getting on with their own lives that they don't spare me a second thought. But ask anybody who has problems with their self-image and they'll say you can't help but worry about what other people think of you. I've learned through my years in racing that if you're in a better place mentally, with things going okay for you, then it's easier to look at yourself in the mirror and be positive. But when you're feeling low – when you're not riding well or your love life is going through the mill – then you can't help but wonder what other people are thinking.

In those first few days at the Isle of Man, my head wasn't right and it was difficult to get in the right frame of mind because heavy rain, sea mist and fog were continually disrupting practice. The first Saturday practice was scrapped because of the rain and the next one, on Monday, saw accidents all over the course, with marshals deciding to go out to escort the newcomers as an integral part of practice.

Both Wednesday and Thursday practices were cut short by bad weather, and by the time it came to the junior race on my 600 all I kept thinking was, *What am I doing here?* The previous year's crash was playing on my mind, I kept thinking of my broken leg and I wasn't enjoying the experience of being back at the Manx. Before heading to the island, I'd spent a small fortune on modifying the bike's suspension and getting it stripped down and in prime condition, yet it wasn't handling well – or at least it wasn't handling well in my head.

I could have easily sat the race out, which was what both my heart and my head were telling me to do. Yet I'd put myself under pressure to compete and I told myself I had to give it a go – I'm no quitter!

I did the first two laps and then pitted but, with no noticeable improvement in either my mindset or the bike, I was all for getting off and walking away. As I came to a standstill in the pit-lane, I started to climb off the bike but Mark Buckley, my mechanic for the event, put out his hands and pushed me back on. "Don't give up now, Maria," he told me, but I shouted at him, "I've had enough, Mark, let me off!" I had my helmet on and was shouting to make myself heard, but he kept me on the bike. I was close to tears and kept telling him, "I don't want to do it, I don't want to do it," but he kept replying, "Give it one more lap, one more lap to see how you get on." I'm not sure how long this went on for, probably only a few seconds, but a pit-lane marshal walked over to ask me if I was alright.

As he was talking, the guy doing the fuel signalled that he was finished and said, "Get ready to go – ten, nine, eight ..." and I didn't have time to answer the marshal, setting off without thinking. I did finish the race, although I came in at a crappy placing, the worst finishing position of my career. But at least it did the trick – finishing the race, however low my placing, seemed to clear my head and make me feel a little bit better about being on a bike. I decided that I was going to race in 2008 and, over the winter, got myself sorted out with a Philip Youles Triumph Dayton 675 and a CMS Honda RVF400. (Of course, I'd also managed to split from Dave and get together with Dominic!)

I got the Triumph to race in the Triumph Triple Challenge – it's a one-make series using race-prepared Daytona 675s with each bike prepped to exactly the same specification, to ensure close and exciting racing. You can adjust the suspension but that's pretty much all you're allowed to do, and with the series consisting of nine races it seemed a perfect way of achieving consistency on a bike which afforded me the same opportunity as the guys I'd be racing against – something that I didn't always get the chance to enjoy in other types of racing, where big teams with enormous budgets will always give their riders the advantage.

Unfortunately, I only competed in the first round of the series before again being sidelined by injury. Even that solitary race at Donington Park didn't go to plan. The track had been covered in snow when I took the bike out for the first time and I crashed at the first corner, Redgate, after my brakes failed. I missed all the qualifying, plus the warm-up races, but I was given permission to start the race itself from the back of the grid.

I worked my way past a fair number of riders to finish 18th, which I regarded as a pretty decent effort, but that was it at far as my Triumph Triple Challenge was concerned. Ahead of the following round I took the 675 testing at Cadwell Park in Lincolnshire, and crashed, breaking my left shoulder blade again!

I'd done that so many times that I didn't consider it a big deal, but I'd done myself no favours by rushing back to racing. I'd really wanted to go to the North West 200, an occasion I always enjoyed, and so I took both the 675 and the

400 to Northern Ireland. However, it was obvious during practice that all was not well with the scapula bone (the one I'd broken at the Manx in 2006) and I couldn't handle either bike well enough to seriously consider racing. So I had to withdraw, leaving me to watch the racing as a spectator from the sidelines.

The shoulder only needed another couple of weeks to heal enough for racing, but with the Triumph series well underway and my season disrupted by injury, I decided to switch focus and race the 400 – only to be hit by engine problems in a round of the Derby Phoenix MCC championship at Snetterton, where I only managed one race and finished 14th.

With the 400 requiring that the engine be rebuilt, it was back to the 675. I returned to Snetteron twice more over the next few weeks to ride well and give my confidence a massive boost. Firstly, I rode in the Thundersport GB, a new series set up by Dave Stewart, the well respected former BMCRC race director who pioneered the MRO Powerbike Tour. I only raced in that one solitary round but managed a very healthy ninth place, and then I had a fabulous time when I went back to the Norfolk circuit that August for a round of the Hottrax TAG UK Endurance series.

I'd been offered a ride in the GB Moto junior team alongside Phil Clarke after Sam Godfrey had pulled out due to injury, but when Phil had to withdraw because of mechanical failure in practice I ended up partnering a 16-year-old lad by the name of Sam Neate, who was at Snetterton to take part in another race. He was a last-minute GB call-up as team principal Mark Smith-Halvorsen scoured the paddock for a replacement for Phil. Although nobody expected anything from our unlikely pairing, we took the 600 class by three laps and finished second overall in the three-hour junior TAG endurance race!

Despite the hiccups caused by shoulder injury earlier in the season, the summer of 2008 had gone far better than I expected. I rode the two events at Snetterton with a smile on my face – the first time I'd done that for a while.

And that smile became a broad grin when I landed a new sponsor ahead of the Manx Grand Prix, with Mark Mann emailing me out of the blue to say that his company, Webtech Software, wanted to support me. That was the perfect fillip ahead of my return to the Isle of Man. With some decent race performances behind me, I began looking forward to the Manx in a way I hadn't looked forward to any race for a good couple of years.

As my racing career seemed to be getting back on track big-style, so my relationship with Dominic began to disintegrate. We hadn't been getting on well in the weeks approaching the Manx, but we'd managed to agree that he'd come with me to the island as both my boyfriend and mechanic. He said nothing to make me think otherwise until the event was almost upon us.

The engine of my CMS Honda RVF400 had been rebuilt following its early season mishap, but I was desperately short of time on this bike, having only recently got it back. I said to Dominic that I needed to test it on the weekend before we set off for the Manx. He told me I'd have to go on my own because his best mate was racing at Donington and he was going there with him. I explained that this was our only opportunity to test the bike, to which he snapped, "I don't care what you're doing, I'm going to Donington!"

This was typical of what was happening in our relationship at this time, so I was like, "Okay, thanks a lot." I got up on the Saturday morning to get myself ready to go testing. He also got up to get himself ready and I said to him, "Have a good time at Donington." To which he replied, "I'm coming testing with you."

Dominic had also told me that it was only 50-50 whether he'd even be coming to the Manx with me; so I told him that, if I was having to go to the Manx on my own, I'd prefer to go testing without him. I didn't really want to believe that he wouldn't come with me because, being so late in the day, I knew I'd have little chance of finding a mechanic or anybody at all to lend a hand. But I didn't want to give him the satisfaction of begging him.

I was living on my nerves; everything was so contradictory in our relationship that I was all over the place. But he came testing with me and we had quite a nice day, so he told me he'd come with me to the Manx. "It's going to be great," he added.

But the day before we were due to leave, we had another argument and he turned round and told me, "That's it, I'm not coming to the Isle of Man." I was beside myself; we were supposed to set off the next morning and he knew how difficult it would be to try to do it on my own. By the morning he'd changed his mind yet again, and so off we went. But I was treading on eggshells the whole time and found it impossible to concentrate on what I was there for – to race.

A fortnight previously, I'd felt so good that I'd allowed myself to think of speed records and podiums. Yet now I was struggling to get a bike on the grid. We had lots of problems with the 675, and every time we put it through scrutineering it failed on something or other. I lost all confidence in what Dominic was doing as a mechanic, and he seemed to spend all his time on his computer or his mobile. If I asked him what he was doing, the snap reply would be, "Nothing to do with you."

It wasn't healthy, but what could I do? I felt awful. If I said anything like, "Would you check over the bike now?" he'd snap back, "Who do you think you are, Rossi?" I told him surely even he could see that things had to be right with the bike if I was going out racing. He'd say he had checked it over, but I was used to people being thorough with my bikes and said to him, "You haven't checked it enough." And the worst thing was that he knew all that, being a racer himself.

Thanks to the Webtech backing, I'd had a lot of work done on the 675 before the Manx, with a new exhaust system and Power Commander (a fuel injection and ignition timing adjustment module) fitted. But I just didn't like the feel of the bike in the limited practice sessions I'd been able to get out on. The weather was some of the worst I'd experienced in my many visits to the island, and most of the practice had to be cancelled because of the rain while the last race of the week, the Senior, was cancelled. When the bike developed handling problems, I decided I had no choice but to withdraw from the junior race.

That left me with just the Ultra Lightweight to concentrate

on. I had my concerns about my 400 bike, having only recently got it back from the repair shop and not having had much testing time with its replacement engine. But it rode like a dream and I finished in a fantastic sixth place, clocking one hour five minutes 30.66 seconds at an average speed of 103.668mph. It was my first finish in this race since my horrible crash of 2006 and, despite all the problems with Dominic, I returned home feeling better than I had done for ages.

(As we travelled back to Brixworth, neither of us realised there was a small sting in the tail. Dominic had caught shingles while we were there, and, as a result, I got chicken pox off him because I'd never had it as a child.)

I might have enjoyed the Manx, but when I returned home my relationship with Dominic really hit the rocks. I started back on the antidepressants again and turned to Tina for help, but her solution was to tell me, "Get rid of Dominic." Although she was right in many ways, I needed more than this at that particular time.

Michelle was a real rock and would invite me up to see her, even taking me to work at Levi's with her. It was thanks to her that I was able to find the strength to make the decisions that I knew were right for me. She was better than any counsellor and was particularly strong when I stopped taking the tablets. I'd always known the tablets were called Fluoxetine, but when I picked up the last lot from the chemist they had the trade name Prozac on the box. That freaked me out – once I realised I'd been taking Prozac, I knew I had to stop. I didn't really want to be taking them anyway, so this was a good wake-up call. I wanted to be in control.

So 2008 came to an end with my racing career seemingly back on track, but my personal life still complicated. Things are never simple with me, but, as I welcomed in 2009, I still felt I had a future as a racer despite the fact the coming season would see me reach my 36th birthday.

CHAPTER 20

PAYING FOR THE RIDE

Because racing is such an expensive business, I've always had to be careful with my money. I guess it's the same in any sport which requires a certain outlay just to be able to take part, but merely getting to the start line is an achievement in motorcycle racing because there is intense competition for a slice of the sponsorship pie. Everybody needs money to go racing and, if they're neither from a rich family background nor lucky enough to be a regular fixture in a top team, then they have to go out and find it.

Some of the resentment I've encountered in the sport has definitely been driven by a belief among some male racers that I get preferential treatment because I'm a woman: the media treat me more gently because I'm of the 'fairer sex'; sponsors give me money because they reckon a woman will get them better publicity; team owners like the idea of having a woman on board because we can help their team stand out from the crowd.

I can see where they're coming from, because when it comes

to landing sponsorship it definitely helps to be female. I've had sponsors give me money purely because I'm a woman competing in a man's world, and they know they're going to get a return on it; at the very least, they'll probably get some publicity whether I win or not.

But it can still be something of a double-edged sword, because the very fact that men see us as something unusual means they have a different approach towards us when it comes to racing.

Roger Harvey at Honda is a really lovely guy, who has sorted out bikes for a lot of racers. But once, when I was after a Fireblade, a powerful bike with more than 120-break horse power on tap and a top speed of around 160mph, Roger was like, "Oh, but I don't want you hurting yourself." I don't think he would have said that to any of the guys. There was nothing nasty in it from his point of view, I just felt as if he'd turned into a father figure and was being protective of me because I was a young female. I don't see that as his fault, it's just the way that society is – the way in which we're programmed to behave.

I've come across that attitude many times over the years. Men see me turn up, they like what a blonde ponytail can give them in terms of publicity and profile, they think over whether they want to give me a bike – and then, somewhere along the line, they remind themselves that I'm a girl, and they don't want it on their conscience should anything happen to me.

I guess that's a fundamentally decent approach, but it does frustrate me and there have been times when it's upset me. All I want to do is race and it shouldn't make any difference whether I'm male, female or anything in between. The only criteria should be how well you can ride the bike – although, as I've aged and mellowed, I do understand that this attitude is driven by the best of intentions.

One of my contradictions is that, even though I have so many problems with my feelings of self-worth and my self-image, meeting and speaking to people I've never met before has never concerned me overmuch. That's probably because I just want to be a good racer. The more people I get to know, the more chance I have of securing the backing I need to do the best I can in my chosen sport.

There are guys in the sport who will treat you as one of them. Chris Barfe is the Honda UK sales manager, and I still joke with him to this day that he's long been the best manager I've never had. He has sorted out so many bikes for me – my three seasons of racing with CJ Bull were thanks to him, and my rides with Cusworths Bikes and Jay 'n' Are Motorcycles were because of the relationship he had with dealerships. He'd always put in a good word for me to get them to supply me with a bike. Both Roger and Chris are nice guys with good intentions, coming at the same situation from different standpoints.

I regard Roger and Chris as mates, but I need to maintain relationships with as many people as I can in the sport because there's no way I could go racing on my own. Taking part in the Manx Grand Prix sets you back around £5,000 when you add up the cost of everything – transport, fuel, tyres, entry fees, accommodation, leathers, helmet, boots and all the kit, spares, chains and consumables. A decent set of leathers will cost you £500 off the peg, but to give yourself maximum protection you need to have them made to measure so you'll pay over double that, while a good helmet will set you back £500.

It's so expensive to race that I come across people who are shocked that I don't come from a wealthy family. In fact, I earn around £12,000 a year from my PR work and, because of the racing, I've never had a lot of time to concentrate on developing a career. From that, I have to pay my rent and living costs and find the money to go racing. There are times when I sit down and wonder how I can manage it. It's a constant juggling act, because I doubt if I've earned much more than £500 in prize money throughout my career.

Fortunately, there are people out there who don't race themselves but seem happy to spend money to watch other people compete. Thank God for them. I was very lucky to meet a guy called Tony Morris, who has been such a fantastic support to me. I met him through Dave when we were still living together, at a time when I was feeling very low about my racing injuries and had little belief in myself.

Tony is a really lovely, down-to-earth guy; his wife Jean is a TT fanatic who knew all about me, which obviously helped. We became friendly and Tony, a self-made man who made his money through a commercial garage in Lancashire, started lending me his motorhome for race meetings. Before long, he also started giving me some financial support for my bikes – culminating in him buying me a BMW S1000RR for the 2010 season. But his support is much more than financial, and we speak pretty much every day. He's a great guy, with no ulterior motive other than he loves his racing.

Unfortunately, some people see such a relationship as something to be nasty about or jealous of. There have been comments put on Facebook or online message boards about how I don't deserve the sponsorship or publicity I'm receiving. Friends have told me I should see that as a compliment, because I've obviously done well enough to rile other people. Their general advice is to ignore it, but it's hard not to let it play on your mind. Over time, I've come to see that it's pointless trying to answer each attacking email or unflattering comment, whereas at one time it would really upset me. There was a spate of it when I was with Dave, and he'd get on the message boards to defend me, but it only gave them the chance to have another snide dig. I'd say to him, "Dave, let's not bother, you're never going to win."

I don't feel singled out because I know it happens to a lot of other people in the public eye, and what we go through is nothing compared to, say, top-level footballers. But there's a lot of nastiness and jealousy out there, and I do wonder about the people who seem to get off on it. Why would you want to spend your entire evening finding fault with people who've never done anything to you? There's so much ranting, and the internet seems to have given a certain type of people a platform for their rage that they probably don't have in any other aspect of their life.

It's not very nice but it's also pretty sad, and I've had to learn the hard way not to let it get to me. And for every negative comment, I get plenty of wonderful, uplifting messages of goodwill and support. Below are two examples of the amazing emails I've received. I've picked them out to share with you because the first one made me laugh and the second one humbled me – please keep them coming!

Dear Top Bird,
Watch out for 4 loonies at the TT this year. We will be sporting the latest 'I love Maria' merchandise. That's if you don't mind me downloading one of your lovely pictures onto a T-shirt. Myself and Crazy Dave did come and try and find you in the pits last year but we think you saw us coming and hid.
Keep it shiny side up.
Mark

Hi Maria,
I thought I'd send a quick e-mail to say thanks ...

I've just (yesterday!) passed my bike test through Steve Guest of Acer training in Gloucester. The thought that you could handle your bikes as you do kept me going when I was stuck on those damned U-Turns ("How do you think small light women control bikes? It's all delicate control!" was a particular favourite of Steve's as I wobbled unglamorously to a stop in the middle of the road for the umpteenth time!)

My girlfriend Kate (who's been biking for quite a few years) booked the DAS for me as a Christmas present and thinks you're fantastic for the sheer guts you show on the road and track. We saw you at the Isle of Man TT in 2005 (a very excited moment for all 6 of us as we realised a woman was taking on the men!!) and again at Donington where you were racing in the North Glos meet at the end of last year.

Anyway, my blathering doesn't seem to be going anywhere, so I'll say thanks again for the inspiration and also for being an idol for Kate!
Good luck for 06!!
Ian

CHAPTER 21

IT'S A TEAM GAME

There have been times in the past five or six years when, because of broken bones or other injuries, my racing has not been going well and I've had to face the thought that my career may be coming to an end. And then I've said to myself, *Flipping hell, Maria, what have you done to your body?*

There are times when, as a result of breaking my hip, leg or ankle, I've had to really concentrate on my walking – I was particularly conscious of how, when recovering from my broken leg, I didn't want to end up with a limp and thankfully I haven't. I feel good about that, because I know my leg doesn't work as well as it did before all the different accidents.

My knees and my right wrist are a bit crummy and I know I'm going to have quite a few problems with them as I get older. I particularly worry about losing the strength in the right wrist, while the various breaks of my collar and shoulder bones mean I'm more round-shouldered than I once was.

I wake up with a stiff leg every morning, but I generally don't dwell too much on my various niggles because they've become part and parcel of me. They're always there in the background and I guess I compensate for them without really thinking about it. At least, while I continue to race, it's better for my confidence if I don't let them bother me any more than they have to.

In my younger days as a racer, I'd plot out my recovery from injury pretty much by instinct. But in recent years I've had a good team around me, particularly in terms of my physiotherapy and fitness training, and I'm hoping it will help me into senior citizenship with the minimum amount of protest from my body.

Even before I became a biker, I'd been very much into my fitness because I'd always been acutely aware of my shape and size. I used to cycle most mornings because I didn't want to be fat and found it an excellent way of helping me to stay looking fit and healthy.

But in recent years I've also had to train to compensate for my injuries, because the stronger your muscles are the better this is for your joints – strong muscles protect your knees, wrists and ankles, among other areas. If I ease up on my gym work then the quad muscles in my legs, for example, begin to weaken – and that means my knees quickly begin to suffer.

When guys meet me face to face, they're often surprised at how small I am. 'Petite' is a word I hear quite often. There's a general misapprehension that bikers have to be big and strong, but it doesn't matter whether you're riding a 250cc two-stroke, a 600cc four-stroke or something even bigger and with even more horsepower, you don't need brute strength to be a racer. I've never bulked up because racing is much more about core strength, stamina and total fitness. The guys at the very top of our sport are scrawny, but they're also fit enough to do the Tour de France. And you've got to be fit to do that, haven't you?

When you're racing, you're not sat still for a moment – you're climbing all over the bike. You never race in a straight line for more than a few seconds so your bum is skimming the seat without stopping as you constantly switch your body weight from side to side. The last thing you need is big muscles to fight against the movement of your bike; instead, you need a body that is lithe, fluid and flexible.

Racing a bike for an hour is absolutely relentless and some part of your body, if not the whole body, is always on the move. People are often surprised to discover that the fitness levels needed to ride in the TT are greater than for many other sports. There are so many different elements – excellent core stability is essential if you're to keep control of the bike, you need good upper body strength, stamina, quick reflexes, a good neck and the ability to withstand a lot of pressure down through your lower legs to your feet. My fitness coach, David Sutton, tries to incorporate all these different elements in my training. As he points out, for some other sports you might need to work on just one element, perhaps your legs or your upper body, but for racers it's a total body requirement.

Of course, one big difference between bike racing and lots of other sports is that you can pay for mistakes with your life. Riding in the TT, for example, is not only physically draining, it requires the highest levels of concentration because one small error of judgement might not only mean that your race is over. There are so many different situations and scenarios; everything is changing all the time as you race and no two races will ever be identical. If you're bunched up one moment, then you've got bikes in front of you and the next they're at your side, you're all going at different speeds and looking to out-brake each other, then one rider can make a mistake that puts other people in danger. You have to take in and compute a huge variety of information and then act on it, which makes fast reactions essential.

Every racer will tell you how difficult it is to maintain your levels of concentration throughout the entire course of a race. There's never one in which everything will go as planned and, as you tire and dehydrate, so your focus can quickly be distracted. I've had times when my foot has slipped off the foot-peg and I've started a trail of thought that goes, *Why did my foot come off the peg? Is that oil coming out of my bike? Am I going to have a slide here?*

You need to quickly get your thought processes back under control before they run away from you. Even when you're doing well, you have to be careful that you don't suddenly start thinking about what you're going to eat for dinner or some other equally random thought. If I find my concentration begin to slacken, I'll start talking to myself, telling myself to think only of what's important at that moment in time. If that doesn't work, I'll get angry and shout at myself to snap out of it.

Getting yourself in the right physical and mental shape to go racing is impossible to do on your own. When I was starting out in the mid-1990s I had the support of some good friends, but they weren't the sort of people to get me working in the gym on my stamina or do anything to help my mental preparations because they had no experience or expertise. They'd encourage me, but only in a general way because they didn't have the specific skills to identify my areas of vulnerability or weakness.

I'm not the best biker in the world by any means, but I've picked up quite a lot of experience just by racing over all these years. But however naturally it comes to you, you can only go so far without the help of people who have a specialised knowledge of the many different parts that go to make up the whole. My racing is now very much a team effort and I'm fortunate to have some good people around me.

I have an outstanding performance coach in David Sutton, who was working as a personal trainer for Fitness First, a gym which has sponsored me for many years, when I first approached him to ask his help in getting my broken wrist working again. Although it's me out there all alone on my bike when I'm racing, I do feel as if David is part of a pretty good back-up team that will hopefully help me realise a few more of my dreams over the next few years.

Toby Branfoot, my surgeon over the past few years, is a top doctor and largely responsible for me still being able to race a motorcycle now. Until I was first referred to him, I'd had no specialist help with recovering from my broken bones, but Toby has a deserved reputation among the biking fraternity as a surgeon we can trust. I can't say I look forward to travelling up to Leeds to see him, because that normally means I've come off my bike, but if I've got to be operated on then there's nobody better.

Once Toby has finished with me, it's my physio Barry Goudriaan's turn. Like David, he's become a friend as well as somebody I can rely on to help me recover as much as possible from any mishap. Barry has probably made me cry more than any other guy I've met, but always for the right reasons, as he works with me to get my shoulder, wrist, ankle or whatever back in decent working order.

As a biker, you're always reliant on the support of other people and there have been plenty of them along the way – so to all the sponsors, supporters, mechanics, cheerleaders, friends and family who have been there for me, thank you very much! I might not always acknowledge it, but your support and love have made me what I am.

CHAPTER 22

GO FOR IT, GIRLS!

The sexist attitudes in my sport will not change until there are more women racing bikes. There are just not enough of us to make any sort of dent to the status quo. Female racers have always been a novelty rather than a force to be reckoned with, ever since the first races were staged on the island back in 1907. The reason the Isle of Man was chosen was because, in 1903, an Act of Parliament introduced a speed limit of 20 miles per hour on the roads and byways of Great Britain, with no exception for racing. So approaches were made to the Isle of Man authorities in the belief they would adopt a more conciliatory attitude to racing on public roads; that assumption proved correct, even if there was the odd hiccup in the early years.

The racing got faster and faster as the bikes got better and better, but it wasn't until well over half a century later, in 1962, that the first woman entered the race – and what a fuss that must have created! Beryl Swain became the first female solo rider in the history of the TT races when she rode a 50cc

Itom to 22nd place out of the 25 finishers. Apparently she wore a colourful patterned sweater over her leathers, with her blonde hair falling out from under her helmet.

If I think I've had it bad in the paddock, how must it have been for this pioneer? And would the likes of me ever have had the opportunity to get on a race bike if it wasn't for her? Not that there was exactly a rush of female racers to follow her out, although by the 1980s there was Hilary Musson, riding in the Formula 2 races on a 347 Yamaha, and a couple of notable foreigners in the West German Margaret Lingham and the Italian Francesca Giordano. Hilary, like Sandra Barnett, had the advantage of a husband already involved in racing, so the door was already at least partway open for her.

There are a few more girls coming into the sport and making their mark, but I can only see further progress being a long, hard slog. Of the roughly four million motorcycle riders in the UK, only around 125,000 are women, and that is a pretty similar ratio to the men and women in racing.

So it seems to me we have two choices – either encourage more women to ride motorcycles in the hope that some naturally gravitate towards racing, or make a concerted effort to persuade some of those 125,000 female riders to take it further than just riding on the road. The problem is, how do we that? Where are the role models for the potential next generation?

Perhaps there is a little light at the end of the tunnel. 2009 saw Carolynn Sells become the first woman in history to win a race over the TT circuit when she won the Ultra Lightweight on a 400 Yamaha. The same year saw Jenny Tinmouth not only take my Isle of Man speed record but also finish on the podium at the British Supersport Cup event in Croft. I can't say I enjoyed seeing my record broken after five years, but at least I got into *Guinness World Records*! I've put Jenny on notice that I intend to take it back, and there's nothing healthier than a bit of competition because it generates interest in us as sportswomen for all the right reasons. It's great that women are starting to get media coverage because they're winning races and beating the guys at their own game, rather than because we've got ponytails or look good in leathers.

I didn't have the best start to 2009 but, somewhat ironically, I really regained my confidence after the TT meeting where Jenny took my record. The big crash at the Manx in 2006 had taken a toll on my body and mind, but by the time I returned to the same event in September 2009 I felt as good as I had done in several years, lapping close to the speed at which I set my record in 2004. That gives me hope for the future and I will, hopefully, play my part in ensuring that us girls give the guys a better run for their money. It was encouraging that, when Jenny went to the TT in 2009, there was actually a little bit of media speculation about whether she was going to take my record. If women's racing becomes something people are looking out for, rather than a sideshow or an afterthought, then that's got to be a good thing.

And we can help each other to keep pushing the boundaries back. Gloria Clark, one of the pioneers of female racing, is a constant inspiration to me and takes her role as one of the founder members of the Diamond MCC (originally the Witch Bike Club) very seriously. With Vivienne Ayres, a saloon car racer, and Marianne Walford, an enduro (mainly off-road) rider, she formed an organisation called Motorsport for Women in the 1990s to support any female involved in land-based motorsport. (Even lawnmower racing!) She's a lovely lady.

I first met Gloria at a race meeting at Brands Hatch and then at the Isle of Man shortly after this organisation came into being, and she has become someone I can turn to whenever I need advice or assistance. She's always in the background, offering her support and encouragement, and it's great to have an older woman with experience of racing to turn to.

I've done what I can to be a role model. In 2007 I was appointed an ambassador for an initiative called RideSafe BackSafe, which worked to encourage young bikers to develop their riding skills through training and to wear the best protective clothing they could afford to buy. It was run by the Lancashire Partnership for Road Safety and Lancashire Constabulary, and also supported by Greater Manchester Police and a number of motoring organisations. It was nice to hear Linda Sanderson, the communications manager for the partnership, say of me that I am "fast, gorgeous and, above all, a very competent and experienced motorcycle rider," and I was glad to play my part in meeting young bikers and helping build their awareness of the threat out on the road.

I've also done my bit through the Women's Sports Foundation. This is basically an organisation that is trying to encourage more girls into sport as part of their healthier lifestyles programme. I got involved when they asked me to come along to one of their big events in Nottingham and speak to an audience of girls about my experiences as a racer. I was put on stage with a number of other women, some of whom told the story of how they'd become involved in their sport. Then this girl stood up and told the most amazingly heart-wrenching story about how she'd overcome a disability to compete successfully, and how she'd been so thrilled to become a coach and pass all her experiences on. Everybody was in tears and I was supposed to be next up. I thought to myself, *How am I supposed to follow that?*

Anyway, I didn't do too badly and they featured me in the next issue of their magazine. I was taken along to the House of Commons where we had tea and cake with the Sports Minister, Kate Hoey. She was very keen to promote more sport in schools and her big idea was to round up a group of prominent sportswomen to motivate girls into emulating them.

I learned an awful lot from just attending these events and watching the other people there. There was the England women's cricket team, athletes, hockey players, Olympic rowers and cyclists; I was the first biker to become involved, which seemed to attract a bit of attention. At one function an MP came up to me and said, "Wow, you race motorcycles!" There is definitely something about motorbikes and women that attracts attention.

A conference was arranged in Peterborough around the turn of the millennium, on a grander scale than anything I'd been to previously. They asked me if I'd do a talk, which I agreed to, and they said they wanted me to ride into the hall on my motorbike wearing my leathers, which I was totally up for until health and safety stuff put paid to it.

So I had to settle for wearing everyday clothes (though slightly smarter than my scruffs) and giving a talk about how, as a biker, I competed in a male-dominated sport. It was after this, as other sportswomen came up to me to chat, that I came to realise how very fortunate I am – almost every other woman there, no matter what they'd achieved in their distinguished careers, had been unable to compete against men and it was a frustration to them. All they really wanted was to take on the men on equal terms yet this was something that they were never going to get. The last thing they wanted was to be treated differently because they were female, and I did start to realise how lucky I was.

I've always been opposed to having separate classes and championships for women in racing. The issue has occasionally been raised, but I always argue that it would be a backward step. Others say that it would encourage more women into the sport, but I don't see how just setting up a second class for females would do that – the likes of myself, Sandra Barnett, Jenny Tinmouth and Carolynn Sells have demonstrated that when women show enough determination they can make their way without being patronised as the 'weaker sex'. I just got off my backside and gave it my all, and girls nowadays have to have that same attitude.

"But you're not a typical girl," are the words that are often thrown at me when I put forward this point. I try to explain that I'm no more special than anyone else, but my love of bike racing has been my motivation. I love the aggression of the sport, the speed, the danger. But a lot of girls will never see it that way. I've taken girls around a circuit on female track days and they tell me how much they want to race – then they go out on their bikes and somebody runs past them up close and fast and they immediately say something like, "Oh my God, I don't like that!" and they want to stop – they just haven't got what it takes to be a racer.

I've seen women try to compete over the years and too often they're just riding around at the back. Okay, there's always got to be someone coming last, and it will often be a man, but too many women just don't want to push themselves. You need desire and commitment if you're going to race competitively, otherwise it doesn't matter what encouragement you give; there are always going to be some women who are suited to it and a lot more who aren't. It's the way they're brought up. Society still very much decrees that girls should take a different path to the guys, but, hopefully, at least as far as racing is concerned, my involvement has helped to change attitudes.

2009 was a really great year for women in motorcycling, probably the best yet, but although the guys will shake your hand and say, "Well done," it's still a case of, "Oh look, a girl on a bike!" It's still a man's sport, and although I have felt more a part of the fixtures and fittings in recent years I still don't think I'll ever be fully accepted.

But that's the price you pay for trying to make your way in a man's sport. Even in darts they separate the men from the women and that's daft – why can't a woman throw as well as a man from around eight feet? Apart from bike racing, equestrianism is the only sport I can think of in which women take on the men as equals.

Perhaps things are changing, but if they are it's only very

slowly and in very small steps. Women have such a long way to go, and for too many young girls it's all about becoming a celebrity for doing nothing in particular. In recent years we've seen this WAG culture that places landing a rich boyfriend or husband above everything else, and I just can't understand why any woman would think that's enough for her.

Personally, I am more feminine than I used to be; I like looking nice and I scrub up okay. But to spend all my time just trying to look my best for a man, to have cosmetic surgery because I think that's what my man might want, to do nothing more with my life than follow a guy around or go shopping ... what a waste. These WAGs might think they have everything but really they have nothing, they're empty. I personally question how that can be a fulfilling life. Perhaps they are the happiest women in the world, and if they are then good for them. But it's definitely not for me.

Girls need to be encouraged to do things for themselves rather than just trying to find a wealthy guy to look after them. I guess that's one of the reasons why the government has tried to get sportswomen into schools to provide some inspiration. You can't change the world overnight, but you do have to start somewhere.

But despite the talk of getting women into sport, we are quite a long way behind many other countries in terms of attitude and the decline of competitive sports in schools has probably damaged girls more than boys. The lads have gone outside the schools for their football or rugby or whatever, while girls have simply given up on sport and got their short skirts on for a night on the town.

If you want more women to take part in sport you've got to be serious about it. You've got to give them the opportunity to try their hands at all sorts, not just in a token one-off PE lesson but on a regular basis. You've got to understand that, as much as taking part should be encouraged, the goal has to be to *win* because that's what sport is really all about. You've got to invest in facilities and quality coaching, but that hasn't happened despite all the big talk. (But then I guess the nation may currently have more important things to worry about than sport.)

I didn't particularly enjoy sport when I was at school, and I do empathise with girls who see it as a lot of hassle for little reward. That's why, when I go into a school to talk to the girls, I will show them the PlayStation game that features me – they seem to think it must be fantastic to be a PlayStation character. I also show them the TV clip of me racing the Porsche, because it's good to show that the girls can beat the guys.

I'll also tell them about the downside to my sport because they have to know that life cannot always be stress-free. I'll tell them about the injuries and the broken bones because you have to expect to come off your bike at some time. And I'll see from their reaction which girls are likely to have a decent crack at sport and which ones would rather worry about the clothes they're wearing and what shade their nail varnish should be. Never underestimate peer pressure – a girl who tries to achieve something for herself can sometimes find herself ridiculed or bullied because she's decided on something a bit different.

I get a lot of satisfaction when a girl comes up to me and

says I've made her believe she can achieve something in sport. But I also find it disturbing to see very young girls content to go down the WAG route who don't want to do anything that might mess up their hair or their clothes.

CHAPTER 23

I'VE GOT MY MOJO BACK!

Five years after becoming the fastest woman at the Isle of Man TT, I was finally recognised in the 2010 edition of *Guinness World Records*. Unfortunately, by the time the book had been published, I'd lost the record to Jenny Tinmouth!

After setting the record in 2004, each year during racing at the Isle of Man I'd keep my fingers crossed that it would remain intact. It was something I was immensely proud of, but I also knew it was not going to last forever. The way Jenny had been racing during 2009, I half-expected her to at least seriously threaten it.

Jenny is a few years younger than me and hers was an amazing effort. On her 1000cc Honda Fireblade, she set a new best of 116.483mph in the Superstock TT and then went even quicker by clocking 116.835mph in the Senior TT.

During the time I held the record, I did some pretty cool things that I don't think would have been possible without it. Dominic may have accused me of dining out on the record, but if I hadn't blown my own trumpet, who would have done it for me? I'm not going to apologise for promoting myself, because that's the way I get to go racing. The record only got in *Guinness World Records* because I made my case to them – it wasn't like anybody contacted me. That's something I advised Jenny to do after she took my record from me – she'll need to make sure that her record is recognised.

But despite seeing the record go, 2009 was an outstanding year for me. After my years of doubt, I got my racing mojo back. By the time the season finished I felt revitalised, refreshed and in the highest spirits I'd been in for a very long time.

The obvious highlight was going to Buckingham Palace to receive my MBE, but I also rediscovered my biking form with my best performance at the Isle of Man in years. There was also a string of other rewarding experiences over the course of a season which didn't start particularly brightly, but which picked up with each passing month until it ended in fantastic style.

My initial plan for 2009 had been to join forces with Derek Redmond for a UK endurance team called Costello Redmond Racing, and our first venture went well as I partnered Jon Leach to second place in the opening round of the Hottrax Endurance Championship. But, because of my work commitments, I wasn't able to commit myself as fully to the team as I needed to – plus we'd agreed that my road racing would always come first.

My plans had always included a return to the North West 200 – I'd fallen in love with the Irish and definitely enjoy being around them, they always seem to have a smile on their faces and want to enjoy themselves even when they're racing hard. Unfortunately, engine failure on a VRS Performance Kawasaki 600 meant my stint there was cut short, although it also allowed me the chance to revisit The Anchor and have a couple of beers with a very amiable crowd.

I extended my Irish experience by going to the Mid-Antrim 100 for the first time and really enjoyed myself in the Supertwins, a class for twin-cylindered bikes up to a maximum of 650cc. It was a typical Irish road race on some very narrow roads, but I felt good on a Team Lynn Suzuki SV650 that had kindly been arranged for me by Darren Gilpin and Paul Lindsey of *Irish Racer* magazine. I finished 12th with a big smile on my face.

I didn't need any persuading to cross the Irish Sea again for the Dundrod 100 and Ulster Grand Prix a short while later. My ride on the Suzuki SV650 in another round of the Supertwins class was just as good as the previous one, and I finished 13th in a race that was staged on the awesome Ulster GP circuit. Unfortunately, I had to retire mid-race in the Ulster GP because of a handling problem. Despite having a 'DNF' (did not finish) registered against my name, I thoroughly enjoyed a fantastic event and I'll definitely be going back. The organisers, with the help of a dedicated supporters' club, had managed to keep the event alive during some very black days in the 1960s and 1970s, when it lost its world championship status, and hopefully there will be many years of productive racing to come at the world-famous Dundrod circuit.

Having enjoyed a big confidence boost, I almost didn't make it back to the Isle of Man for the Manx because a deal I was being offered for a bike proved too expensive for my meagre budget. However, I agreed a last-minute deal with another TT rider, Davy Morgan, to ride his CSC Branson Yamaha R6. I was able to race, although I was bitterly disappointed with the starting position given to me by the organisers. I'd sent off my application as normal, but when I got my notification through I found they'd given me the starting number 48 – I hadn't been put that far down the field in years. I couldn't even bear to have the letter around me as a reminder, so I put it back in the envelope, tucked it away in a drawer and tried to forget all about it. I felt very disheartened, because they obviously didn't think I could ride well anymore.

During practice week, if you put in a good lap time it's possible to get your number changed but the weather was against me. It rained a lot in that first week and that, combined with frequent fog, meant practice was often cancelled, leaving me very few sessions when I could go fast. I didn't bother asking to get moved up the field because I was sure they'd turn me down, so I just tried to get my mind in the best possible shape for the junior race.

It's at times like these when having good people around you makes all the difference in the world. Davy Morgan is an Irish guy with so much cheek it's frightening, and he was fantastic, telling me, "Don't let your start number fry your head – just forget about it. Yes, you're going to have a lot of traffic, but it's going to make for a great race and you're going to catch them and pass them – catch them and pass them ... You're going to enjoy doing that, so get it into your head and start thinking about that instead of moaning."

And that's exactly what I did in the race – I don't know how many people I passed, but I was flying. It felt fantastic, as good as it had been for some while. But halfway through the second lap my right arm started pumping up – because I'd had so little time on the bike I hadn't got a proper feel for it and had been gripping too tightly, with the result that the wrist I'd previously broken began to swell. All the old negativity started whirring away. I began thinking to myself, *I can't hold onto this, I can't carry on,* and I started to look for somewhere to pull over. *Don't talk yourself out of this one,* I kept telling myself, *you're doing well.* But I was also in danger of talking myself out of the race by the time I got to the pit-stop.

My team were fantastic. The moment I stopped they were fuelling the bike, but I was looking around for Davy because I wanted to let him know how I felt. I spotted him in the pit-lane and gestured to him that the bike was moving about a lot, but all he said was, "Yeah it will be – just get on with it," in his typically cheeky style. I grinned and set off.

Steve Caffyn was doing my fuel for me and obviously overheard this conversation, so I also had him telling me, "You're doing well, you're doing well!" That was ringing in my ears when I set off, but I wasn't sure whether he was just saying it. Still suffering from all my doubts, I overshot the bottom of the hill at Quarter Bridge, overshot at Braddan Bridge and then messed up at Union Mills. I was beginning to undo all the good work I'd done earlier. *What the hell are you playing at?* I demanded of myself. Looking ahead of me, I couldn't see anyone to try to reel in, so I told myself to chill out, relax and enjoy riding the R6. I got back into the flow and my arm wasn't really hurting all that much, so I told myself to use the bike and savour the experience of riding the TT course. I managed to talk myself back into the race and did well enough that, on the fourth lap, I set my sights on a couple of the guys ahead of me and managed to claw them in.

Then, as I came up the return road at the finish, I saw my mechanics clapping me, I pulled into the holding area thinking to myself, *There's not many bikes here – perhaps I have done okay.*

As I sat on my bike, I saw Richard Freeman running towards me. Richard has been involved in racing for donkey's years and I've known him from back when I used to do the CB500s in a support class at British Superbikes. "Would you like some help?" he said to me,

"I'd love it!"

Richard isn't a mechanic or anything, but he's great to have around for moral support and he really knows his stuff. He seems to know everybody inside and outside the paddock, he knows how racing works, he knows when to talk me up, when to calm me down and how to comfort me if I'm in need of it.

He's an absolute diamond, everybody loves him, so when I saw him running towards me with a big smile on his face I hoped he would be bearing good news. "You've finished 17th and you've done 115 miles per hour," he breathlessly told me. It felt good. "And you're the first girl home," he added. I nearly leapt off my bike in a Frankie Dettori moment. Carolynn Sells had started 13th on the road but the news that I'd beat her on time, plus my higher-than-expected finish, was like a booster injection. My confidence and self-belief came flooding back. Lots of people came up to me to say things like, "That was mega, Maria!" "We weren't expecting that!" "It's great to see you back!" It was all good stuff, and it felt nice after all the doubts that had followed me around since that awful crash at the Manx.

I walked away from the paddock, telling myself over and over, *I can ride again.* It felt so good – this was what I'd always wanted to do, after all.

I wanted that feeling to last forever, and I was still feeling great when I went out a few days later for the 400 race. Perhaps I wasn't as nervous as I should have been, maybe a bit too relaxed, but I couldn't get worked up by having to start further down the field again – even though I saw Carolynn starting six places ahead of me. I gave her a nod of the head and told her, "Have a good race," and I must say she looked really confident. But I felt good too.

The start was delayed by the weather and a lot of the top boys dropped out because of bike problems. I'd only made it to Kerrowmoar, around 20 miles into the race, when mine packed in. Because I hadn't had much time to test the bike, I feared it was the engine packing up again, but thankfully it was only the fuel pump.

I stood at the side of the road with a marshal who had his radio on for the race commentary, when I heard, "Carolynn Sells is now into the lead." I thought to myself, *She's going to bloody well win this!* The commentary continued. "She's not coming in for a pit-stop, she's going for a four-lapper, this is history in the making!"

The marshal turned to me and said, "Fantastic, isn't it?"

"Yeah, absolutely brilliant."

"It should have been you, though, shouldn't it?"

"Do you think so?" I'd so wanted to be the first girl to win a race at the Isle of Man, and now that opportunity had been denied me – forever.

I was freezing cold because I'd stood by the side of the road for pretty much the entire race, but the course car picked me up to take me back to the paddock. As it drove around the circuit, it started to rain, which was just what I didn't want because I was due out next on the 600. It took a long time to get back to the paddock because we had to keep stopping to pick up riders. During the ride back, the guys were saying the race was going to be postponed because it was really lashing it down on the mountains. They all seemed agreed that the weather was too bad for racing. Yet, as I climbed out of the car back at the paddock, the clerk of the course announced via the tannoy system that the race was being brought forward half an hour – which meant it would get going pretty much straight away.

My head was already a bit fried because of Carolynn becoming the first woman to win at the Isle of Man, and I really could have done with a day to get over that – just a little time to come to terms with the fact that it would never be me, and to enable me to move on.

Instead, it was a frantic rush in the paddock as we scrambled to get ready to go out again. Davy Morgan had been out on his 250 and finished third, so he was in the beer tent when I wanted him around to lift my spirits. I dashed back to my van to pick up a few things. I was nervous by the time I got back to the paddock and my mechanic, Maurice Hogg – another great Irish bloke, who used to race until he was quite badly injured – must have seen that. He came up to give me a big cuddle, and he said, "You don't have to go out if you don't want to – we're all really happy with what you've done this week."

Everybody was the same, they were so nice, and I started crying again. But then Davy turned up and told me, "You *are* going out – of course you're starting the race." He told me to stop my flipping crying, but there just wasn't time for me to clear my head. I literally just got to the road, sat on the bike and off I went.

I set off fine, got my head down and passed loads of people. But then I came to a section where the rain was chucking down. I had brand new dry tyres on and, as the road became slippery, so the bike began to slide all over the place. I asked myself if, having just got my confidence back, I really wanted to go and lose it again in the same week. I was convinced that they'd have to red-flag the race and call it off because of the rain, so when I got to Parliament Square I decided enough was enough and pulled off the course.

Although the race wasn't stopped, it was the right decision for me. The rain kept moving around the circuit, which made it a nightmare for the riders as they didn't know what conditions were like around the next corner. I wasn't going to stick my neck out, and I wasn't the only one because a lot of racers were retiring into the pits. However, I couldn't bring myself to go back to the pits straight away. I think I wanted to be on my own and to gather my thoughts for a bit, full of the contradictions of knowing it was the right thing to stop but still feeling as if I'd let myself and the guys around me down.

Then Michael Sweeney, another of the Irish guys, jumped Ballaugh Bridge so high and fast that when he landed his exhaust shook loose and fell off. He got black-flagged and, as he pulled in at Parliament Square to retire from the race, we ended up sitting and chatting together. "I'm gutted, gutted," he said.

"Look, you're here to fight another day," I felt able to tell him.

"I should have carried on."

To which I replied that they wouldn't have let him. But they would have let *me* carry on if I'd wanted, so by the time I got back to the pits it all seemed a bit of an anticlimax. I'd felt so good a few days earlier and this wasn't the way I'd wanted it to end.

I didn't go to the beer tent and only went to the awards ceremony as it was coming to an end. All I really wanted to do was pack up and head off, but instead I went to Colours, a nightclub, with all the guys from the CSC team. I let my hair down, had a great laugh, and felt very much at home in their company.

Those guys look after me so well that I only wish I'd hooked up with them years earlier. We all went out for a meal on the last evening and Tony Morris came along as well. There were around 20 of us and Tony paid the bill, which was well over £500. He stood up and said, "That's for Maria, because I know how lovely you've all been to her." Everybody looked at me and I started crying, but it was a lovely moment and I felt good to be a part of that crowd.

That wasn't the end of the season for me, however, because things were to get even better before 2009 came to an end.

In between the North West 200 and the Mid-Antrim 100 a few months earlier, I'd ridden in the Four Hours of Spa Classic at Spa-Francorchamps in Belgium. This is an event that involves a team of two racers sharing one motorcycle built prior to 1 January 1980, with no rider able to race for more than two thirds of the distance. I'd teamed up with Mike 'Spike' Edwards on a Chris Wilson Offenstadt Kawasaki and, although the bike was plagued with problems, we had a fantastic weekend of racing and managed to cross the finish line in 52nd place, which was something of an achievement for that machine!

Chris had said to me in Belgium that he'd arrange for me to take part in the Goodwood Revival in September, which I thought would be amazing although I didn't want to get my hopes up. Held over three days, it's a fantastic event in the motorsport calendar that sees some tremendous racing in an entertaining, nostalgic atmosphere.

Tickets sell quickly and there's always a clamour to be part of a unique event, so I told myself that if Chris got me in there he'd be my very own *Jim'll Fix It* and Father Christmas rolled into one – and that's exactly what he is. I got an entry form from the organisers through the post, got accepted and set off in September, still pinching myself to think I was to be the first girl to race in a Goodwood Revival. It was a wonderful three days.

It was a glorious sunny day when I arrived. After scrutineering, we headed off to the cricket match being played in the grounds by Lord Marsh and some of his mates, as well as some of the celebrity drivers and riders. There was a massive marquee where you had tea and cake and Pimms, and we made a champagne toast to Stirling Moss to mark his 80th birthday.

Everybody was dressed in period costume and it was like stepping back in time, surrounded by historic cars, motorbikes and aeroplanes. Because I was racing I had access to the drivers' club, which had been done out like an exclusive 1950s-style canteen. Inside it was like a who's who of racing – people like Wayne Gardner, who had 18 wins and 51 podium finishes in his century of 500cc Grand Prix racing, Jamie Whitham, a double British champion twice voted Man of the Year by readers of *Motorcycle News*, 'Pocket Rocket' Leon Haslam, Chas Mortimer, who won eight Isle of Man titles in the 1970s and 1980s, and Phil Read, known as 'the Prince of Speed' after winning 52 Grand Prix races and other titles all around the world.

There were many more legends old and modern. I teamed up with Roger Munsey – who rides the Norton Domiracer owned by Chris on a regular basis – for the four-hour endurance race as part of the Barry Sheene Memorial Races. It was all very different for me – the gear change was on the wrong side and it was all very vibratory – but we had a great time. It was not only a lot of fun, but we also finished 13th overall and ahead of Phil Read – yes, that's Phil Read MBE, eight-time world champion, noted in *Guinness World Records* for winning the most 250cc world championship titles.

It was the first time I'd been on a classic bike and I raced against Chas Mortimer, who came up to me afterwards to tell me, "You're not a bad rider." A little while later, at Silverstone, I bumped into another old rider, Paul Smart, who told me that Chas hadn't shut up about me – it felt cool to have such a legend speaking so highly of me.

Although I generally feel happier when my parents don't come to watch me, I did take them to Silverstone on that occasion. To try to make them feel a bit special, I arranged VIP hospitality and introduced them to some of the riders and people in the paddock. It was a bit strange, as I think lots of people who know me had come to assume I didn't have parents. Mum was so excited that, when I took her to breakfast, all she wanted to do was take photographs, get autographs and talk to the riders whose names she'd come to know. I got a friend to pop them around on the back of a scooter and they bumped into John McGuinness. He couldn't get away because Mum wouldn't shut up, telling him how much they loved him, how they were his biggest fans, how they had pictures of him in their kitchen, how I'd got his autograph for them. John told me about all this later and I stood there thinking, *Hang on, I hadn't even heard all this!*

Then I went off to France with the editorial team from *Ride* magazine, on their last big trip of the year before their test bikes had to be returned to the manufacturers. I had a great time socially as well as getting to ride some wonderful bikes around the roads of Normandy. As the curtain came down on the 2009 season, I found myself looking ahead with more anticipation and optimism than I had for many years. I might have hit my mid-thirties but I'm young at heart and determined to make the most of the time I have left for racing.

CHAPTER 24

NOW I CAN MARRY IN ST PAUL'S!

To say that my MBE came out of the blue is an understatement. I wasn't expecting anything like that in a million years.

Because I've lived in so many different places, I've always had my post sent to my parents' house in Spratton, and so one day in the late spring of 2009 I popped round to pick it up. Mum wasn't there, but Dad pointed out one that looked very official and asked me if I'd been caught speeding! I opened the envelope to find a letter telling me I'd been nominated for the MBE, basically asking whether I would accept it.

My first instinct was that this had to be a mistake. Or a wind-up. I read the letter again, it was all very official, and I still couldn't believe it. I gave it to Dad to read and he said, "Oh my word, we'd better not tell your mum – it says here that you've got to keep this in the strictest confidence."

I said that if it were true, there was no way we could keep it from Mum.

"You know what she's like," he said, "she'll never be able to keep this secret."

"Yeah, you're right," I laughed.

Dad insisted it seemed genuine, but all I kept thinking was, *Why me?* What had I done to become a Member of the Order of the British Empire? I read the letter again and thought that perhaps all it meant was that I'd been placed on a list of people to be considered for an MBE, not that I was definitely getting one.

Despite the warning of keeping it in the 'strictest confidence', I asked a mate to come round and showed it to her. "You're definitely getting it," she said to me, "there's a box here for you to tick to say you'll accept it." I slept with that letter next to my bed and each morning I'd wake up and read it, thinking of how special it would be if it actually happened. While I'd half-expected my TT record to go to Jenny Tinmouth, getting that letter couldn't have come at a better time. It took some of the sting out of the fact that I wasn't the fastest woman at the TT anymore, something which had been a massive point in my life.

Anyway, we had to tell Mum and by the end of June it had been announced officially. Mum made sure everybody in the village knew and a whole lot more people besides. With me able to take three guests along to Buckingham Palace, it had to be her, Dad and Tina, who all began seriously planning their big day out in November.

They'd wanted to go down to London the night before the ceremony because we'd been told to arrive by 10:20am on Tuesday 17 November, but I said we'd drive down in the morning. Any hotel in London would cost a fortune for us all and just be extra hassle. Also influencing my decision was the fact that I'd only got my outfit sorted out the day before in something of a last-minute panic.

I'm not exactly a footballer's wife when it comes to clothes, and I've never been a great one for shopping. On the Saturday before I was due to collect my MBE, my friend Bonnie Lane, a very good photographer, called me to say she wanted to come to London to take pictures of me at the Palace. She asked what I'd be wearing and I told her I hadn't got anything sorted out – what did she think I should wear?

I think Bonnie was a bit taken back, and she said she'd see if she could put me in touch with the person who had styled her for her wedding – if you've seen Bonnie's wedding pictures, you'll know why I was happy to hear that. Her friend Cath gave me a call later that day to say she wasn't going to have time to come to Northampton and shop with me, but she gave me a few pointers and ideas. My initial thoughts were that, when going to the Palace, a lot of people dress as if they're going to a wedding with big hats and suits – but that isn't really me, I'm not too formal, and Cath told me to avoid this sort of get-up. "You're too young to be doing that," she told me, which I was pleased to hear. She checked out the pictures on my website and I emailed her a few more, then she called a little later to tell me to go shopping and buy everything that caught my eye, take it home and see what went together. That's how she does it as a stylist, she told me – and I could return everything I didn't use.

So I spent all day Sunday at Milton Keynes, which has one

of the biggest shopping centres in the country, looking for dresses and accessories. I went to one of the personal shoppers in John Lewis, but what she was getting me to try on was awful – I just ended up politely saying thanks but no thanks. I went back home with this one dress – at £200 it was the most expensive item of clothing I'd bought for myself outside my racing leathers – and when I tried it on I looked in the mirror and thought, *I don't even like this very much*. Even if I wore it to the Palace I'd never wear it again. Did I really want to spend that much money on a dress that I actually wasn't that keen on?

So, less than 24 hours before my date with Prince Charles, I had nothing to wear. And then I had a stroke of luck. Cath rang me on the Monday morning to say she was coming to Northampton to see some worktops for her new kitchen; while she was here, she'd also come over to help me get myself sorted out. She didn't get to my home until lunchtime but immediately started going through all my clothes, sizing each item up with a yes, no or maybe as she threw them on the bed. She asked me what I liked in my wardrobe and I showed her a short black jacket, which she said was a great piece.

"But now we need to go shopping to get all the accessories you need. Have you got any shoes to wear?"

I had to admit I didn't – what sort of woman am I?

We went to Northampton town centre and Cath took me around the shops until they shut, buying all sorts of jewellery, shoes and other bits and pieces. She took me back, dressed me up, and I felt great. To have somebody like her doing that for me was exactly what I needed.

I didn't even get to wear the £200 dress. Instead, I went to the Palace in a little black £20 dress that I'd bought from H&M and had already worn many times that year. We dressed it up with a Chanel-looking jacket that was actually from Top Shop, and the jewellery we'd bought, while we also went for a bow in my hair rather than a big hat.

I'm not like my mum and sister, or probably most other women, when it comes to clothes. Mum had been thinking about her outfit for months before the day. She wore a gold jacket with a hat that looked amazing, and Tina had a posh new outfit on. Even Dad had got himself sorted out well before me, buying a new suit. But I was happy with my budget effort, although it took me a whole day later in the week to take back all the things that I'd bought with Cath – as well as the £200 dress.

We had to be at the Palace by 10:20am, so I told them we'd leave Northampton around seven o'clock, which should have given us plenty of time to make the roughly 60-mile journey. Mum, Dad and Tina all came to my apartment, the first time we'd seen ourselves in our outfits, and we set off in my little Ford Focus.

Tina was in a bit of a mood to start off with, so the car was a bit quiet. We got down the M1 without too much hassle, but as we hit the A5 to go into central London the traffic was at a virtual standstill – pedestrians were walking quicker than we were moving in the car. The clock seemed to speed up and I began to panic that we weren't going to make it on time. Dad was sat in the back, warning us, "We're going to miss it," and Mum was snapping back, "No, we're not, we'll be fine!" Tina and I were sat in the front watching the clock. Mum said to me, "Your clock is fast," and I was thinking to myself, *Yeah, but not* that *fast!*

We still weren't moving, and it got to the point where I had this horrible feeling that – having gone through all that build-up since receiving my letter back in June – I wasn't going to get there. *Maria, you're a disaster,* I told myself as I tried to fight off a rising sense of panic. What had I been thinking of when I decided not to go down the night before? And when I decided to drive down instead of taking the train?

We were crawling through Cricklewood in north London with no sign of the traffic easing. I turned to Tina and told her that we weren't going to make it.

"Oh my God!" she said. "Don't let Mum hear, because this is more important to her than anything else in the world."

It was then that I just turned round and informed them, "I'm really sorry, we're not going to make it in this car, but I really don't want to miss it so I'm going to ask a friend to help me get there."

"Can't your friend get us all there?" Mum asked.

"No," I replied. "Four of us won't fit on his motorbike."

I'd known Damian Rowley for years through racing. He'd started riding on an RD350 in the early 1990s but, after a series of injuries, had retired in 1999. We'd been back in touch in 2009 and, a week or so before my trip to London, 'Demon' had been up to see me in Northampton on his Virgin Limobike, which is basically a motorcycle taxi service. I said to him that I still hadn't been on the back of the bike and he told me to give him a shout whenever I was in London so he could pick me up and ferry me around – a far quicker way of getting through the capital's traffic than any car. So I texted him to say I was stuck in traffic, I wasn't going to make it to the Palace and could he help?

Whenever I'd been to London before we'd hadn't met up because he'd always been miles away, on the other side of the river. But this time I got him just as he was finishing a job not too far from where we were still crawling along; he told me to park up and he'd find me. I explained I had the family in the car and we'd carry on crawling, but, just a few minutes later, he came riding up as I leaned out of the driver's side window to wave him down.

I pulled the car in by the side of the road and got out, with Dad getting in the front to drive. I gave him a kiss, waved goodbye to Mum and took my heels off, with Tina stuffing them into a bag for me while I put on my little flat shoes. Damian gave me a helmet which I put on, I got on the back of the bike in my little short dress and he kindly preserved my modesty by covering me in a big apron – which made me laugh because the company I do my PR work for, Bagster, sell them and everyone is always taking the mickey out of them. Yet I've never found a more helpful piece of equipment in all my life!

Whoosh! We were off, and I hardly had time to say goodbye to my folks. Tina told me later that both she and Mum started crying as I raced off, leaving Dad to the driving duties. After a few minutes on the back of Damian's bike I was hit by what I'd done, and I started crying too. Damian was really good; via the helmet intercom he kept telling me that what had happened wasn't my fault, but I didn't want to hear that – my family had so wanted to be there with me and I'd messed it up.

We were flying down the A5 and, after a couple of miles, the traffic began to ease. Damian said I'd definitely make it and there was a good chance my family would as well, so I had to hold myself together. We arrived at the palace gates at exactly 10:20am and the police waved him up, telling him, "We were expecting a bike."

But not this bike, I thought to myself, *this wasn't planned.* But we weren't going to tell them that. "Do I look alright?" I asked Damian as I got off the back. "Yeah, great," he smiled back. I thought, *No, I don't, you liar, my dress is all creased, my hair's all over the place and my makeup has probably run because I've been crying.*

Damian got a call to his next job and, after telling me to "enjoy it", he whizzed off. It was only after he'd set off that I thought that I should have sent him to get my dad and bring him in, but I just wasn't thinking straight. Instead, he left me standing across the gate from these two policemen, feeling like a bit of a lost sheep before one of them shocked me by grinning and saying, "Hello Maria." I was like, *But how do they know who I am? This really is getting quite surreal!*

They were absolutely brilliant. "Am I too late?" I asked them as I checked my watch again; they said no, but that I should go straight through. They saw me getting my heels out of the bag to switch shoes and told me to keep the flat ones on because it would be easier to walk on the gravel.

The letter informing me of the procedures for the day had warned that, if I was bringing any guests, then we all had to arrive together. I explained to the policemen that my family were in the car but I'd left them on the A5; they said that if they got there quickly they'd send them through. So I rang Tina to give her the good news.

"But Dad's gone the wrong way and we're lost," she said.

I didn't really want to think about Dad driving in London traffic in a pressure situation. When I asked where they were, Tina said she wasn't really sure; they'd just hit a load of roadworks and were stuck in them. As I was talking to her, I went to walk into the Palace but one of the policemen said to me, "You're not allowed through with your phone."

"But my family are lost and I'm trying to help them get here," I told him. "Can you speak to them?"

So I introduced him to Tina and he took my phone, found out where they were and started to guide them in. The other policeman asked me for some identification and I had to confess that I'd forgotten my passport – which had dawned on me when we were sitting in all the traffic on the A5 (after I'd spent the previous few days nagging my family to make sure they brought their identification) – but thankfully he accepted my driving licence. And so I walked off, leaving the other policeman chatting away to Tina on my phone.

With all this happening, I hadn't had much of a chance to think about what was about to take place. So I walked into the Palace, still the little lost sheep, and I found my way to the cloakroom, touching up my makeup and doing the best I could with my hair. Then I was put in this room with everybody else who was there to receive an MBE – I was the last one in, and the door was closed. I'd made it by the skin of my teeth, though with my mind on my family I hadn't even started to enjoy the experience.

I took a glass of water and told myself to start making the most of this – when was I likely to be invited to Buckingham Palace again? Then this nice lady, who was also there to receive an MBE, asked me whether my family had come along with me. That was enough to set me off again, despite trying to prevent the tears running down my face and ruining my makeup even further. I told her the story of our morning and she was telling me to be positive, that they would make it, but I'd given up on that because, even if they got to the gates, they wouldn't be allowed through.

We were called for a briefing and this guy came to give us our instructions, slipping into the conversation that we'd be meeting Prince Charles, not the Queen, which caused quite a lot of the people there to have a little grumble. Not me though, I didn't care because I was still in a bit of daze.

There were around 150 of us in the room and, during the briefing, we were told that we had to walk up a certain way: curtsey (for women, obviously) – walk back three steps – walk forward three steps – and curtsey again. We were told what to say and what not to say, how to address Prince Charles, and a few other things that seemed to be going in one ear and out the other. I was trying to remember what I could and to squeeze in one last practise of my curtsey, because I was wearing heels – which I never normally do – and was worried that I might fall flat on my face in front of the Prince.

We were put in line and moved through to another room for a few minutes before we eventually got to go downstairs, in the correct order, to walk through the back of the ballroom where it was all going to happen. I looked into the audience and was thrilled to see Tina and Mum and Dad sitting there. Suddenly, I was the happiest person in the room! As I looked into their beaming faces, I realised how important it was to me to have them all there. Somebody said to me later that it would have been a bit like getting married without having your parents there, and that was how I felt. It was one of those events which was as much about them as it was about me.

We lined up in a queue to meet the Prince and I was surrounded by these older ladies who all seemed absolutely petrified. Personally, I wouldn't have cared if I was stood there in my leathers, I was just so happy for me and my family to be there. The lady in front of me was trembling with nerves and I told her not to worry, because if anything was going to go wrong that morning it would definitely be something to do with me – I'd be the one most likely to trip and fall over him! I only said it to try to calm her down and make her laugh, but I thought to myself that, what with everything else that morning, perhaps I shouldn't be chancing my luck.

I was desperately watching the people ahead of me, and I could see a lot of them were making mistakes in how they walked up to him and the way in which they turned. So when it got to my turn I had to walk a few feet and then stand square on. Just before you walk up to the Prince, there's a guy standing there who whispers in your ear, "Do you remember what you've got to do?" I said, "Yeah, I think I'm okay." And then he said to me, "You're the biker, aren't you?" adding,

"You look very nice." He sent me off to meet Prince Charles with a grin on my face.

I walked forward, turned, did an adequate curtsey, turned to face him, walked the three steps – got it all right! Finally I was in front of him and it was, *Oh my God, it's Prince Charles!* He was lovely; the first thing he said was, "So did you come by motorbike?" and I replied, "Actually, I did." He laughed. I told him a little bit of the story and it did seem like a really long time that we were stood there chatting, although it must have only been a minute or two.

He asked me whether I intended to carry on racing, and I said, "Gosh, yeah! I know your sons are really into their motorbikes too."

"Oh yes, very much so," he replied.

What I should have said was that, if they ever wanted to go racing, they could have a go on my bike, but I missed the opportunity. Damn!

Then I had to walk backwards, curtsey and go through to another room. I got taken to one side by the Press Association to do an interview and they asked about our conversation. I was in one of my dazes, it took me a moment to recall what the Prince had said and so I told them the story of how my morning had gone. It appeared in all the papers. Then I went back to sit in the audience and watch the remainder of the people getting their turn; I caught my sister's eye and saw Mum waving like mad – apparently, when I came through they'd all started crying.

I couldn't wait to find out how they'd made it. After the formalities were over, they told me how Tina had directed

Dad by following the instructions of the policeman with my phone. They'd pulled up in my car at the palace gates and one of the policemen stuck his head through the window to ask them, "Are you the Costellos?" They were ushered through the gates and directed to park up against the palace wall, just outside the door. Then they were rushed through and helped to their seats; I'm so grateful to those policemen for making sure they got in and treating them so kindly.

When I went back to the gate to collect my phone, I thanked them massively for getting my family in. I also met Bonnie, and she took some pictures of me with the policemen and with the family, then I got called back inside because a guy from the Irish press wanted to do some pictures – I was walking in and out of Buckingham Palace like it was my home!

By this time, everybody had started taking their phones out to call friends or family from the Palace or to sneak quick pictures. We all went to the toilet because everyone wants to use the loo at Buckingham Palace; the queues were massive. I took a picture of the toilet and when I came out Tina, who was next in line, asked me if that was the flash from my phone; we had a good laugh when I told her, "Yeah."

Mum and Dad were still beaming, we were all happy, and we went outside to queue to have our photograph taken together. We were told to fill out a form, but I said to my family that we didn't really need it – they cost an absolute fortune. Mum insisted, but then a photographer from the Press Association asked if he could get some pictures of me with my family. I asked if there was any chance we could have some prints and he said he'd sort it out for me. Dad was so excited he was taking pictures of virtually anything that moved – or stood still! (When a coach and horses came through the gates it got the full treatment.) Then the Press Association did a video interview with me that went out to TV news stations and over the internet.

We drove out of the palace gates and headed off towards the Mall, where we met up with my friend Hilary from school. She works at Marlborough House as an archivist at the Commonwealth Secretariat, so we went into a nearby pub for some lunch. I was standing at the bar, waiting to get the drinks, when this guy across the room said to me, "You looked really nice today, congratulations." I turned round and said, "Has Mum been talking about it?", thinking she'd already started telling everyone in the pub about our day. But it turned out that this guy – and the two others he was with – had been standing behind Prince Charles wearing the fancy costumes and holding the ceremonial spears. So they stayed and had a few drinks with us before we headed back to Northampton for a family meal. When we were sat in the restaurant my phone didn't stop beeping, with all this stuff on the internet coming through about me. It seemed to be on every major website: the BBC, *The Times, The Telegraph*, *The Mail*, the specialist press, the lot. And then the text messages of congratulations from friends started coming through; it all made for such a great day.

Yes, there had been a lot of drama and it could have been such a disaster, but it ended up a fantastic day, something for Mum and Dad to really get their teeth into and tell everybody about. I've got a friend who works at *The Independent* and he said he'd keep an eye on the news wires to see if any pictures of me came through – the first one he saw was one of Prince Charles laughing with me!

Now, whenever I go home to Spratton, Dad greets me with, "Hello MBE." He's got this little bag of goodies from the day, with the investiture booklet, some pictures and a few souvenirs that he must have taken to nearly every house in the village. Whenever I see him he tells me that he's been to see so-and-so and they need a signed photo – him and Mum are absolutely loving it. I had a friend over from America to stay recently and Dad told him that they now have to bow whenever I walk into the house!

I've had a few people say things to me like, "So why exactly did you get it?" and I have to admit that even I'm a bit puzzled. Motorbike racing is something I love, it hasn't exactly been a hardship, I've just followed my heart and done something I enjoy – and it's landed me with an MBE! But I'm getting used to explaining to people why I *think* I got it. Though I doubt if I'll ever know who nominated me, the honours list is full of sportspeople. I guess all the different governing bodies are putting their people forward to get their sports recognised.

All my friends have been absolutely fabulous about it. I recently caught up with some friends from school who I hadn't seen for years. We met in a pub near home and I had my MBE in my bag because I'd just come from my parents, who'd had the extended family around to see it. They all wanted a picture with the MBE and my friend Katie, who is a doctor, was with a new boyfriend who wanted his picture taken with me to show to some friends who knew me.

When I was at school I went around with some of the most intelligent people in my year, although I really wasn't one of those. Yet here they were, sitting in a pub going, "Wow, look at you!" and I'm saying, "Yeah, who'd have thought that I was the one to get an MBE?" Certainly not me!

The only slight downer was something nasty that was put on one of the internet message boards, saying that I hadn't done anything to deserve the award and suggesting that a petition be started up to have it taken away from me. The person kept their identity a secret, but I suspect it was a former boyfriend who got pretty unpleasant when we split up.

I've grown a thicker skin in recent years, but you still can't help but wonder why some people have to be so nasty. There have been times when I've felt surrounded by envy and I'm well aware that there are a handful of people who enjoy it when I fail. Because of the way I am, it can make it quite hard for me to be pleased or proud about anything I achieve. I started to tell myself that perhaps I didn't deserve my MBE, but luckily my family and friends have put me straight on that.

One consequence of my MBE is that it entitles me to marry in St Paul's Cathedral, although this was something I only discovered after I met this American racer at the TT in 2009 and we were flying backwards and forwards to see each other. It went so well that, in early 2010, we had this incredible seven-hour conversation on Skype in which we chatted about pretty much everything, including the apparent myth that MBEs could marry in the same chapel as Prince Charles had wed Diana back in 1981.

The relationship had become quite intense by this time – I guess a seven-hour video-phone conversation gives you a clue as to that – and the conversation touched on us getting married. Not because of anything to do with love and all that, but because it would be amazing to get married at the place where Charles (my buddy!) and Di had tied the knot – what a venue!

It was so exciting just to talk about the prospect that my female imagination got carried away, to the point that I emailed St Paul's asking whether MBEs could actually marry there. Two days later I received an email back, saying that they could! It also contained loads of information about everything from the type of musicians I could book to the best florists to use. When I told my boyfriend about this we actually started discussing how close to the 2010 TT we could do it.

I sent another email to St Paul's requesting availability, and got a reply which was formal and straightforward until I got to the last couple of paragraphs, which read:

"On a completely different note, my partner and I go to the Isle of Man each year for the MGP and always made a point of watching you ride and think you are wonderful. When you had an 'off', during practice week (I think) I can't recall the actual year, Fred (my partner) and I took an orchid plant to Nobles Hospital which we handed to the staff asking them to hand it on to you to let you know people were thinking of you and wishing you well."

The email was signed *"best wishes from Joan,"* and her orchid is still going strong to this day at the home of my good friend Hilary Holdaway on the Isle of Man. I'd often stay with

Hilary when racing on the island and it was during stays at her home that I set my speed record and then later broke my leg.

After that accident, while I was recovering at Nobles, I woke to find this orchid by the side of my bed but I couldn't think of anyone I knew called Joan. It had remained a mystery until I received the email.

The orchid had been given the name 'Maria' by Hils. When I went to the Isle of Man for the TT launch early in 2010 I got reacquainted with it – it's huge and still flourishing! I told Hils the story – we both had a laugh at how I had to get an MBE and fall for an American mad enough to consider marrying me, before I could even find out who had sent me the orchid years previously!

CHAPTER 25

CARRY ON RACING!

I was born in 1973 and started racing when I was 21, although I haven't always been honest about my age. When I was approaching my 30th birthday I guess I began to see myself as getting on a bit, so I started telling people that I'd been born in 1977, immediately cutting four years off my age and taking me back to my mid-twenties!

Funnily enough, nobody else at that time seemed bothered about how old I was. Now I know I'm getting older because this is something people ask me about more and more.

I tell them that I intend to carry on racing for as long as I can – it's all I've ever wanted to do. It's certainly never brought me great fortune: I've never owned a house; I drive old bangers; I've never been able to develop a career because racing always comes first; most of the time I've raced other people's bikes. My sister used to moan at me, saying, "Why don't you buy some new clothes instead of spending all your money on racing?"

"When you find something you want to do, you'll work it out," I'd tell her.

I've spent all my money – and a lot of other people's – on my racing, yet my dad is always saying to me, "You live the life of Riley – when are you going to get a proper job?"

I've worked hard over the years to support my racing, in more ways than one. I do a bit of writing, a bit of TV work, PR, stunt doubling ... pretty much anything that will give me an income. I couldn't have gone racing without earning money because it's very expensive to run a bike. It's not like an athlete running – if you've got a bike you need a van to get it to the meetings, you need fuel to get there, fuel for the bike, tyres, entry fees, leathers, helmet, boots and all the kit, spares, chains and consumables. You can never have enough money in this sport unless you get in with one of the biggest teams.

I've had enough injuries to know that there will be consequences to my long-term physical wellbeing too. I'll probably be a bit of a mess in my old age. My handwriting has deteriorated since all those problems with my right wrist, and I do have problems with my shoulders and ankle.

But I've been very inspired by some of the guys who have been seriously injured, some much more than me, and overcome it. Iain Duffus is a good pal who was one of a select few to win the TT, the Ulster and the North West before retiring a few years ago; he had loads of injuries and overcame them. Every time I had a crash he'd be saying to me that he thought it was time I packed it in. I'd reply, "Why? Look at you – you're taking all those painkillers and you're still racing."

Mike Doohan, who was five-time Moto GB world champion and such a legend that he's been placed in the Australian Sports Hall of Fame three times, is an absolute hero of mine; his lower leg was so weak towards the end of his career that it bent when he was racing. Mind you, he's a millionaire so he'll be alright when he's older – but who'll be looking after me when I can't get about?

That's where all my hard work on my fitness comes into it. I try to be as fit as I can not just for racing – it plays a big part in keeping me together and moving. If I can't move – like when I've been trapped in my room because of injury – I don't feel alive, and that's when depression can kick in.

I'm a doer, a fidget; I need to be busy; I must have goals. Racing makes me feel I'm somebody and nothing is going to take that away from me. I might not have always done as well as I'd have hoped, but I think I've done okay. And I think I've shown that I'm not the sort of person to let injury get in the way of achievement or ambition.

I doubt if my parents will ever completely come to terms with my racing, and I know Mum still worries every time I set off for a meeting. But the MBE has definitely changed her attitude and she sees it in a different light now – she might worry about me but I know she's also very proud of me, and that makes me feel good.

It wasn't too long after I received my letter of notification that I lost my Isle of Man TT speed record to Jenny Tinmouth in 2009, and that hurt much more than I was prepared to let on at the time. I spoke to Tina about how I felt but didn't say anything to Mum. Tina must have told her, because the next day she rang me and said, "You've had that record for a few years, Maria, and you can get it back."

And I'm thinking, *Blimey, that's Mum basically telling me to go faster!*

It's taken a long time, but she's right. I can go faster. I can get that record back and I am not going to give up racing. My plan is to carry on racing until I can race no more.